M000308647

ICONIC SUMMER CAMPS AROUND JACKSONVILLE

Iconic SUMMER CAMPS AROUND JACKSONVILLE

Dorothy K. Fletcher

THE
History
PRESS

Published by The History Press
Charleston, SC
www.historypress.com

Copyright © 2021 by Dorothy K. Fletcher
All rights reserved

First published 2021

Manufactured in the United States

ISBN 9781467148214

Library of Congress Control Number: 2021937213

Notice: The information in this book is true and complete to the best of our knowledge. It is offered without guarantee on the part of the author or The History Press. The author and The History Press disclaim all liability in connection with the use of this book.

All rights reserved. No part of this book may be reproduced or transmitted in any form whatsoever without prior written permission from the publisher except in the case of brief quotations embodied in critical articles and reviews.

CONTENTS

INTRODUCTION

*I*n an earlier, gentler time, when Ike was still president and television was still a new contraption, Jacksonville's children spent a great deal of time outdoors. During the autumn, winter and spring, groups of "boomers" would roam the neighborhoods after school in search of kickball games or rounds of tag or hide-and-seek, and they would go inside only when they were called to dinner or the streetlamps came on.

During the magical time of summer, kids discovered the "wilder outdoors" offered by the summer camps of the northeast Florida area. These children had a variety of camping experiences from which to choose. There were camps for kids in Boy Scouts, Girl Scouts and Campfire. Some kids had an opportunity to go camping with their church youth groups to campsites owned and operated by their denominations. Some kids went to a kind of camp offered by museums for art enrichment or to universities for band camp. Some campers went for the day, and sometimes they went for weeks at a time. When these children got a bit older, they became counselors and guides, because some part of them had been transformed by the beauty of a northeast Florida pine forest or the magnificence of a sunrise over a lake soon to be filled with raucous swimmers.

This book will provide the history of numerous camps, but certainly not all of them. Some seem to exist only in memory, but the ones I write about had either well-documented histories or innumerable people who had memories to share. Over one hundred people responded to my call for memories and photos. I was actually quite surprised that just mentioning summer camp generated so much interest. Everyone who contacted me had summer camp experiences, and they either loved camp or hated it. Everyone, however, wanted to share their stories. Some memories are funny—and some are quite poignant—but all of them were meaningful and precious.

Since I signed the contract in the middle of the Covid-19 pandemic, I did not realize that gathering information was going to be so difficult. The Downtown Public Library was closed for some time, and when it opened again, a stringent schedule for researchers had been instituted. This meant that I did not have the usual instant access that I had enjoyed when writing earlier books. The internet proved very beneficial to me, as did telephone interviews, which proved invaluable for getting information. I also gleaned a great deal from many willing campers on social media.

Early in my research, I made an executive decision on how to organize the wealth of information that I found concerning the camps of northeast Florida. I determined that the best way to order the chapters on camps would be alphabetically. This may not feel as historical as it should, but many of these camps began at or near the same time. Since all of them were often occurring simultaneously, I didn't want to show any sort of favoritism. Ordering camps alphabetically seemed the fairest way to go.

I also felt I needed to discuss the cultural part of camping—the gear, the food, the songs and the fireside tales. Chapters on these aspects of camping will be interspersed between chapters on camp histories. Hopefully these asides will provide readers with a deeper insight into the histories. I hope that readers will find this book illuminating and satisfying as it guides them on a journey to recall many wonderful (and sometimes not so wonderful) camping experiences.

Finally, I decided to address each camper by his or her first name, rather than by last name. Many times, I felt as if I were interviewing young campers and not full-fledged, adult human beings. I observed a certain joy and youthfulness in the recollections of the people with whom I talked, and writing this book has been a delightfully energizing experience for me.

I am certain that northeast Florida readers of a certain age will relish a walk through these memories to the happy, challenging times of summer camps—the campfires and the scary stories, the nature walks and the wildlife, the swimming lessons and contests, the handmade arts-and-crafts treasures and the water journeys in canoes. If nothing else, we learned about the delight of s'mores and the joy of getting a package or letter from home. In the end, the most important lesson we learned was how wonderful going back home could be after we had braved the rigors of summer camp and had come back all in one piece.

CAMP BLANDING

I promise to do my best to…
Report for duty on time
Perform my duties faithfully
Report dangerous practices
Obey my teachers and officers of the patrol
Strive to earn the respect of fellow students
Strive to prevent traffic crashes by always setting
a good example myself

—AAA School Safety Patrol Pledge

I never would have thought of Camp Blanding as a place where children would get to enjoy summer fun. I always thought of it as a place for soldiers and war games, but I received two emails from men who remembered very fondly their time camping at Camp Blanding as kids. It seems that in the '50s and '60s, boys, in particular, were rewarded for their hard work as AAA School Safety Patrol Boys—assisting in directing traffic around school campuses and helping children safely cross busy streets. Many boys were rewarded with a trip to Washington, D.C., but others were given a chance to go somewhere closer.

I began to search for information about this particular summer camp by going online to the website of Camp Blanding Museum. The website said that Camp Blanding was formed after the sale of Camp Joseph E. Johnston (later known as Camp Foster) to the federal government. The land once known as Camp Foster became the site of the Jacksonville Naval Air Station because of its strategic location on the St. Johns River. The Armory Board used the money from the sale to buy a site on Kingsley Lake for a training facility near Jacksonville. They eventually acquired twenty-eight thousand acres between December 1939 and November 1940 either by purchase or by eminent domain condemnation. The WPA (Work Projects Administration) helped construct fences and roads within the camp and also helped install water and sewer lines.

At first, the War Department wanted the camp to accommodate a regiment of infantry, but with the Second World War threatening in early 1940, the government decided to increase the capacity to an infantry brigade. The camp was named for Major General Albert Hazen Blanding, former commander of the 31st Infantry "Dixie" Division and chief of the National Guard Bureau.

According to the website, Camp Blanding played a major role in World War II by training the 1st, 29th, 30th, 31st, 36th, 43rd, 63rd, 66th and 79th Divisions. The 508th Parachute Infantry Regiment and the 6th Cavalry Regiment also trained there, as did three tank destroyer battalions, field artillery regiments and combat engineer organizations. In June 1943, the camp began preparations for a change, and in August of that same year, the last divisions left and the camp was converted to an Infantry Replacement Training Center. Almost 175,000 men trained at the IRTC.

Camp Blanding also served as a German prisoner of war camp from September 1942 to April 1946. There were more than four thousand of these prisoners—soldiers, U-boat sailors and civilian "aliens."

I made a trip out to the museum, which is most impressive and located today just outside the gates of Camp Blanding. One would not be able to tell that inside the unassuming building, there would be fascinating exhibits, photographs and artifacts of the soldiers and reservists who had trained there. No information on schoolboys or summer camps, however.

The next day, I interviewed George Cressman, the historian at Camp Blanding Museum, on the phone. He also had no information about young boys using the camp in the summertime, but that didn't mean children didn't get to be there. We deduced that kids could have camped there, however, between wars and conflicts. Between World War II and the Korean War and between the Korean War and Vietnam, Camp Blanding was relatively quiet, so it could have been used in the summers by Patrol Boys. Imagine it, Kingsley Lake nearby and so many interesting places

102—"Attention" on Company Street, Camp Blanding, Fla.

© CURT TEICH & CO., INC.

Soldiers at Camp Blanding, 1942. *Courtesy of the Florida State Photographic Archives.*

where soldiers had prepared for combat. Camp Blanding had to have been a young boy's paradise.

David Miller seemed to think so. On May 7, 2020, in an email he sent me about his time at Camp Blanding, he wrote:

> *In sixth grade I somehow managed the grades to make the School Patrol. In those days, trips to our nation's capital were not even on anyone's radar. Instead, we were rewarded with a weeklong camping trip to Camp Blanding. We stayed in the military barracks and had our meals in the Chow Hall. As I remember we had the run of the camp and spent our days swimming in Kingsley's Lake. For a bunch of 12 year old boys (girls were not on the School Patrol in those days, maybe it was too dangerous). It was the adventure of a lifetime getting to spend your days away from home living in a military setting and eating military food in the "Chow line." Great fun!*

On June 5, 2020, I received another email about Camp Blanding from an old classmate of mine. Patrick Hinely started off by saying that his camp experiences began during the summer of 1963, after sixth grade at San Jose School #83 and before seventh grade at Southside Grammar, School #7, where his mother had also gone to school. He said:

13

For our school year of public service, members of the School Patrol were rewarded with a week at Camp Blanding, on the shores of Kingsley Lake, under the watchful eye of the two Duval County Sheriff's Officers who supervised the county-wide program. They were joined by several high-school and college-age counselors, a couple of whom taught us some new words.

Us San Jose boys shared a barracks with the guys from South San Jose. It was my first time away from home on my own for such a long stretch, but any anxiety about that was eased by being able to gaze over Kingsley's waters and see my great aunt's lake house, where I had been going, since early childhood, to revel among a huge and loving extended family. From there, for as long as I could remember, I had looked across to this very part of Camp Blanding where I was now headquartered.

The food was memorable, though not as haute cuisine. I'd bet money that some of the military surplus foodstuffs we were given, such as the huge vats of peanut butter on every table in the mess hall, dated from the days when new GIs were passing through Blanding on their way to

The Museum at Camp Blanding, 2020. *Author's collection.*

World War II. It spread easily on the plentiful white bread. Try as I might, I don't remember the jelly.

We slept on cots in long barracks with screened open sides above about three feet of unpainted cinderblock wall. There was no ceiling, only the beams and joists holding up the plywood roof. Except for not having a floorwalker's cage, it was reminiscent of the prison barracks in Cool Hand Luke. *My family home in Lakewood did not yet have air conditioning, so adapting to the summer temperatures and humidity didn't faze me. I remember the breeze off the lake feeling nice, as did swimming in the lake, which we did twice a day.*

Heat and humidity were the excuses about half of my fellow campers— in retrospect, most likely the ones from homes with air conditioning—used to leave early and go home. I stuck it out. It's still the only time I've ever stayed overnight on a military base.

It may not be written anywhere that young boys got to camp at Camp Blanding, but as long as memories serve, the youthful times at Camp Blanding will live on. Summers spent there certainly had to help young men develop skills and talents they didn't know they had—roughing it outdoors, away from home and the sometimes-smothering influence of family. Those times still live vividly in the memories of many.

CAMP CHOWENWAW

On my honor, I will try:
To serve God and my country,
To help people at all times,
And to live by the Girl Scout Law.

—*Girl Scout Promise and Law (1984)*

As I drove the twenty-two miles from my house to Green Cove Springs on August 5, 2020, to conduct an interview there, I couldn't help but recall my first time as a camper at Camp Chowenwaw in 1960 when I was ten and going into the fifth grade. My parents had saved enough money for me to go to summer camp as a junior Girl Scout. With my little suitcase and pillow, my parents deposited me on the grounds of the camp, kissed me goodbye and then drove away. I remember a feeling of elation filling my heart. This was it! I was free of their rules for two whole weeks!

That feeling lasted only until Bonnie, one of my cabin mates, arrived. She was a mass of tears, sobs and sniffles, and her family hadn't even left yet. Her mother began to weep and her father teared up, and soon I could feel my lower lip begin to quiver as I witnessed this sorrowful display.

As I recall, some counselors came along and divided Bonnie from her parents swiftly and with great efficiency—whisking the parents in one direction and the child in the other. I stood alone in my uniform shorts and shirt outfit my mother had recently purchased for me, and I tearfully realized I would be without my mother's caring presence for fourteen

Girls arriving at Camp Chowenwaw by automobile, 1930s. *Courtesy of the Clay County Archives.*

whole days. As the chaos of campers arriving and tearfully waving goodbye to their families whirled about me, I stood alone, feeling a cold sense of foreboding creep over me.

At my lowest point, however, my other cabin mate, Ruth, stumbled up to me with all her gear. She was a down-to-earth, confident sort. She laughed as she boldly dropped her things and came up to me and, with hands on her hips, said, "Aren't you excited about camping here?"

"I am now!" I replied with a grin, and my camping experience was saved from disaster. A kindred spirit had approached me, and things really looked up for me from then on.

Back in my present reality, however, I realized I had missed my turn and had to make a U-turn on US 17. Eventually, I saw the gate to the camp next to a new housing development. I drove past the houses and right through an unremarkable gate where the camp began. Quickly, I found a shady spot and parked. That is when something amazing happened. The place surrounding my car was still huge, and that surprised me.

Often when I revisit my childhood haunts, they look small and decidedly unimpressive, not at all as I remembered them—but that was not the case with Camp Chowenwaw. The trees towered over me as my field of vision filled with a riot of green colors. I felt small again, as if I might be ten years old, and that was weirdly nice. As I exited my car, the air on that summer afternoon was heavy with heat and humidity, and I could feel myself fall back into a distant time some sixty years past, when life without air conditioning was the norm and summer camp was the great obligatory adventure for most kids in earlier generations.

Liza McCain, education and volunteer coordinator at the ranger's station, met me near the gate, and before she became busy with administrative tasks,

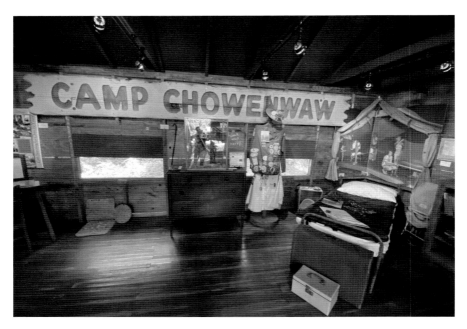

Above: Camp Chowenwaw Museum, 2020. *Author's collection.*

Opposite: Graffiti left by campers at Camp Chowenwaw, 2020. *Author's collection.*

she unlocked the Camp Chowenwaw Museum for me and gave me sole and unlimited access to wander about and take pictures. It was amazing!

The museum was one of the old cabins that had been relocated to the front of the park. It had been refurbished and outfitted with Girl Scout paraphernalia and artifacts from earlier camping generations. Instead of four cots, as a regular cabin would have had, there was only one on display, angled from a corner so people could walk around it. On it was a bedroll and sashes of Girl Scout badges. A leather suitcase and cosmetic case stood at attention at the foot of the bed as if some camper had just arrived. In one corner, there was a desk and chair for writing and an old radio on the writing surface.

Posters of the Girl Scout Promises and Laws hung from the walls as well as newspaper clippings for special events. These were preserved in frames. The saddest for me was the clipping for the Closing Ceremonies in 2005, when Camp Chowenwaw stopped being part of the Girl Scouts organization.

There were bookcases filled with old handbooks and song books, and there was a pie safe filled with all manner of camping cookware and lanterns used by girls of long ago. There was even a scale model of the Big Cabin on

display. But the very best things to see were all the names and messages from past Scouts drawn, written or painted on the wall. "Pam (Smiley Face) was here. 2004" "Cait hearts Ryan!" "Tina R WUZ hErE!"

As I stood there in the cabin, I could almost hear the giggles and the whispered gossip of many generations of girls who had been housed in this very space. As a matter of fact, I could have been in this very cabin with Bonnie and Ruth, although I couldn't find my own graffiti, which I am certain I would have carved or written. Even though it was an old building, it still contained a youthful vibration, and it made me unusually uplifted.

My next stop was to the Big Cabin, where Liza took me in her golf cart. The Big Cabin was and is the heart of the complex, and its story is as old as the camp's. Liza provided me with a copy of that history written by an unidentified Girl Scout Council member of a much earlier era. It is titled, "The Story of the Building of Camp Chowenwas [sic]," and according to the history, the camp began in November 1932.

The Girl Scouts of Duval County apparently were interested in and had some funds for a summer camp facility. In November 1932, they were informed that they could secure federal aid in the building of a camp for the Girl Scouts. That assistance was in the form of labor, and the council realized then that they could better afford to meet their goal of building a summer camp if they could supply the land and the materials for buildings. Federal money would provide the manpower and pay for the labor.

The federal agency that would have provided this labor was undoubtedly from the Works Progress Administration, an agency formed by Franklin D. Roosevelt to help men find work during the Great Depression. The part of that organization that would probably have come to Chowenwaw was the Civilian Conservation Corps (CCC). The website www.u-s-history.com said of the corps, "The Civilian Conservation Corps (CCC) was a program designed to address the problem of jobless young men aged between 18 and 25 years old."

In the months that followed, there was a frantic search for a suitable place to build a camp. They finally decided that a six-acre parcel in Green Cove Springs, Florida, would be the place. (I believe this fact might be an error or a typographical omission, since the historical marker on the property says the original purchase was for sixty-seven acres). The older document went on to say:

> *Negotiations were begun with Mr. Dunn* [the real estate agent] *for its purchase. We learned that "our place of property," as we were calling it now, had been owned by Mr. Simon Williams and used as a dairy farm. He had lost it in a foreclosure mortgage to the Peoples Bank. When the Peoples Bank failed Mr. Dunn became receiver for the Bank and now he was offering the land for slae* [sic].

View from the entrance of Big Cabin at Camp Chowenwaw, 2020. *Author's collection.*

In January 1933, the council finally held the deed to the property. They procured Hobern Smith as architect, who used the council's rough sketches as the basis for his plans. G.L. Lewis was put in charge of the building project. He went to the property several times to be sure that there were enough pine trees to build the type of log cabin desired. As a cost-saving factor, the

Completed Big Cabin, 1933. *Courtesy of the Clay County Archives.*

builders were to use the trees on the property for the whole project, and they even set up a sawmill run by a tractor on the site.

Originally, the council wanted a large building in which to assemble the Scouts and for use by troops in the winter. In the summer, they had planned on using tents as sleeping quarters, but it was later decided that small wooden "huts" would be better, and they could use the "waste lumber of the log cabin."

Then, on January 17, 1933, at the height of the Great Depression, the first truckloads of laborers (about 150 men) entered the property to begin clearing jungle-like growth. Soon the sound of these workers chopping and felling trees filled the woods. They would soon be making walls, raising roofs they covered with whittled cedar shingles, chinking the logs of a big log cabin and making magnolia wood furniture. The regular building crew consisted of 50 to 60 men. These men were put up in Jacksonville and trucked to work in Green Cove Springs every day. T.C. Burbridge and C.E. Ward were the two foremen. Ward lived in a nice bungalow on an adjacent property provided by a Mr. Dunn. Ward was to keep an eye on the project and keep it secure.

The hope had been to open the camp in May, but it wasn't until June that the last of the clay chinking was completed. There was a celebration for the workers with a wiener roast using twenty pounds of hot dogs and all the fixings. On July 1, 1933, there was an event for the entire Girl Scout Council to examine "one huge log cabin for living and dining, three units of five cabins each, one bathhouse, one cabin for hospital, one cabin for doctor, and one cook house, one cabin [*sic*]. One board walk one-fifth mile long out to the build [*sic*] in swimming pen, and innumerable pieces of outdoor furniture, for a real house warming."

One interesting side note is that the Kiwanis Club had provided money for the bathhouse, and forever after, it was called the "Kiwashi" in the club's honor. As a camper at the camp, I was under the impression that it was some sort of Native American term, albeit the word *wash* is right in it. (I was only ten.) I was incredulous when I discovered that the word's true meaning was actually a play on the name *Kiwanis*.

According to a display in the Camp Chowenwaw Museum, the Big Cabin was condemned in 1973, "due to the deterioration of the logs and

Interior of Big Cabin, 1930s. *Courtesy of the Clay County Archives.*

under-structure." There was such a tremendous outcry within the Girl Scout Council and from many past campers that architect Ted Pappas was approached. He recommended that the Big Cabin be restored and offered to do the renovations. The Meninak Club of Jacksonville provided funds for the work on the Big Cabin and funded a new kitchen as well.

I got to speak to Ted Pappas about the renovation in a phone interview on October 1, 2020. He said that he had a "great time" working with the Girl Scout Council members. This was a "fun period" of his life. He had graduated from Clemson, joined in the service for several years and then became an architect. He was part of a business community where he joined other young architects like Robert Broward, Taylor Hardwick and Peter Rummell; each set up an architectural firm in a row of old houses that they had renovated on May Street.

What Pappas remembers most about the renovations of the Big Cabin at Camp Chowenwaw was how deteriorated the building was. Wooden structures are hard to preserve under the best of circumstances, but a wooden structure in swampy Florida is not going to last forever. He also recalled that they had to use a great deal of wood to make up for all the years of neglect.

The display also said that after the renovation of the Big Cabin was completed, the "Meninakitchen" was dedicated in July 1975. The camp website said that thirty-one years later, in 2006, the Big Cabin complex was again in need of a major overhaul. This time, it was Clay County, Florida, and Kenneth Smith Architects that were able to make the needed repairs and preserve this magnificent building.

There is a marker in front of the entrance of the latest version of the Big Cabin that reads:

CAMP CHOWENWAW

Created in 1932, Camp Chowenwaw (Cho'-wen-waw) derived its name from the Creek word for "sister." Prominent Jacksonville resident Nancy Osborne, with the support from local organizations such as Rotary and Kiwanis Clubs, led to the effort for the Girl Scout Council of Duval County to purchase the 67 acre parcel at the mouth of Black Creek for $250.00. This newly acquired land served as the camp's grounds. Federal help to build camp structures came from Reconstruction Finance Corporation during the Great Depression. One of the biggest jobs was the construction of the Big Cabin, including shingles and furniture from timber harvested on-site. Swedish granite, originally used as ballast in

Archery practice at Camp Chowenwaw, 1930s. *Courtesy of the Clay County Archives.*

19th Century sailing ships, was donated by G.W. Parkhill and used to construct the cabin's fireplaces. The camp expanded in 1951 by adding another 40 acres. For over 70 years Camp Chowenwaw enriched the lives of young women by providing them a place to master new skills and talents as Girl Scouts. The camp remains an important part of Clay County history and serves as a county park offering recreational activities in a preserved natural environment.

A FLORIDA HERITAGE SITE
SPONSORED BY THE CLAY COUNTY HISTORIC
PRESERVATION SOCIETY
THE CLAY COUNTY BOARD OF COUNTY
COMMISSIONERS AND THE FLORDA DEPARTMENT OF
STATE

fF-874   2015

My guide, Liza, said that the original swimming pool, which would be ready in 1933, was placed in the clay pit from which the chinking for the logs of Big Cabin came. This hole was perfect for a pool, so an artesian well was drilled. The Girl Scout history said that "the day the water gushed from the artesian well was as richly celebrated as a gusher of the West."

This original pool had (and still has) cement walls like a swimming pool, but instead of a cement bottom, it has a sand bottom at one end and a bottomless pit at the other (at least no one found it when I went to camp there). It also had something that other pools do not have, and that was

Camp Chowenwaw's Big Cabin, 2020. *Author's collection*.

wildlife. When I was a camper, there were little fish and tadpoles in the pool just as a lake would have. It was also rumored that under the little diving dock, water moccasins lived. We were repeatedly instructed never to go under there, but just the thought of encountering a snake meant that most girls would go nowhere near the dock, much less under it.

Liza took me to this original pool, which is now a true pond, complete with reeds and turtles and fish. The edges of the pool that served as walls still stand and hold the water and wildlife in, but one would have a hard time swimming in this pool. There are many grasses and reeds growing against the sides. A fountain pulls water from the well and sprays it into the air, and turtles drift about like little moving islands.

Immediately, I recalled all the raucous cheering and shrill counselor whistles that were part of swimming activities at Camp Chowenwaw when I was a camper there. To think that I had swimming practice in this space is just amazing. In later times, this pool would be used to teach girls how to right overturned canoes before they were allowed to canoe in the river. I never got to canoe or even right one because my swimming skills were rudimentary for my entire time at camp.

Right: Swimmers in the clay pit swimming pool at Camp Chowenwaw, twentieth century. *Courtesy of the Clay County Archives.*

Below: Clay pit swimming pool at Chowenwaw, 2020. *Author's collection.*

Today, in a different place of the park, there is a beautiful Olympic-sized pool for people who visit. The water is turquoise and clear, and the only wildlife is that of the students of a local day camp.

Liza's tour took me past the new additions of tree house cabins that are elevated screened-in cabins the public can now rent when they camp there. She also pointed out the Tree House Trail that was built by the "OD 39

Co A 3/20 SF Fla ARNG Green Berrets [*sic*]" in 1977 and marked by a large granite marker commemorating their contribution. We finished off the tour when Lisa allowed me to walk the length of the Jungle Trail on a wooden path that runs along Black Creek on the camp's property. The newly renovated trail was completely surrounded by thick foliage, and after about a quarter of a mile, the river became visible. Somewhere near this point, canoes would have put into the water.

I enjoyed a satisfying trip home. As I drove along, I was able to put together the reality of a place with what I remembered and found that I wasn't too far off the mark. Camp Chowenwaw is as impressive a place as I remembered—as impressive a place as I have ever known—not only because it was part of my youth but also caring organizations have kept it from sinking back into the wild or into the ravages of a strip mall or housing developments.

Soon after my trip to Camp Chowenwaw Park, I went through all my interviews with women who had once been part of the Camp Chowenwaw, the Girl Scout camp. Cindy Mathieson is one such camper. We spoke on the telephone for quite a while about Camp Chowenwaw on May 26, 2020, and she had so much to share.

Cindy began attending the two-week session of Girl Scout camp at Camp Chowenwaw when she was about eleven, between her fifth and sixth grades. Here she could enjoy swimming, canoeing, crafts and square dancing. She remembered that there were six campsites on the property where large groups of girls were each assigned for two-week periods. There were two kinds of sleeping arrangements—platform tents in some campsites and the original wooden cabins built by the CCC during the Depression in the others. When it was time to eat, the troops would march to the Big Cabin (also built by the CCC). Each group was named for different Native American tribes—Abanaki, Iynu, Yamasee—and each would sing its unique chant on its way to and from the "mess."

There was the Kawashi, the bathroom, and there were Kapers (This is a play on the term "K.P." or kitchen patrol) to be performed—chores that each girl had to do during a certain period. The crafts were another thing that filled the girls' time. They worked with leather and made key chains. There was also wood burning and "sit-upon" making—a sit-upon being a device made from oil cloth and newspaper, laced together to form a mat to "sit upon."

Cindy told me that swimming initially took place in a spring-fed clay pit, the clay from which was used to chink the Big Cabin. The pit was turned

Campers checking out Kapers chart at Camp Chowenwaw, 1965. *Author's collection.*

into a pool with a sandy bottom in the shallow end and a bottomless floor at the deep end. (Actually, she told me, that was where the spring was). There was a dock at the deep end, and campers were warned not to go under there because water moccasins often went there. The campers preferred the part where the pollywogs (tadpoles) and minnows stayed.

Later, in the '70s, a modern pool was put into the camp ground, but the old swimming pool remained and served thereafter as a place to take the "Tipsy Test"—a test to be sure one could right her canoe and get back in should it roll over. She told me that no one was allowed in the river until she could pass the Tipsy Test.

Cindy also had stories about the wildlife at Camp Chowenwaw. Along with the pool creatures, there were scorpions and roaches and mosquitoes.

She never, not even once, saw an alligator; however, she did see raccoons, and she told a great story about a group of raccoons she encountered:

> *During the school year, when the camp catered to weekend Scout troop visits, the raccoons in the forest would congregate on Friday night, as if they had been waiting all week for campers to come. They were probably drawn by the smell of cooking and s'mores. First, one would make his way down the paths to the campfires. Then another would come close behind. Soon a mother and her kits made their way forward, and the whole group had to be shooed away. The troop leaders thought it best that any trash needed to be locked inside the Big Cabin or else the raccoons would make a midnight raid of campsites for sure!*

There was another memorable incident she shared. It was a near tragic event that happened in the summer of 1977. She was a camp counselor then:

> *Square dances were being held in the Kiwita, a screened pavilion on the campground. It had been raining most of the day, but the girls were still having their lessons since being in the Kiwita meant they all could stay high and dry. The hour came for us to head back to our campsites. We dispersed, singing all the way home, and all of us made it back to our cabins when a huge pine tree fell and crushed the Kiwita flat! Thankfully, not a one of us was near the structure! It could have been disastrous.*

On May 5, 2020, I spoke on the telephone with Janice Lynn, who now lives in Indiana. She told me that she lived in Jacksonville in the early '70s, when her father was stationed in Jacksonville with the U.S. Navy. She was a Girl Scout at the time, and she went with her troop to a performance of *Holiday On Ice*. She just happened to be in the right seat, because she won a two-week summer camp stay at Camp Chowenwaw in Green Cove Springs. "I remember laughing so hard at some of the things we did and talked about. I had the best time. I had a roommate who was homesick, though. I was not very sympathetic. I kept thinking 'How can you be homesick? It is so much fun here!'"

She also said many of the people there were so kind. Her best recollection of Camp Chowenwaw occurred near the Fourth of July. "I remember we had a Fourth of July celebration where we reenacted the Boston Tea Party, and we often went canoeing in the St. Johns River. We would go past so many swampy places. I kept my eyes peeled for alligators. Never actually saw one."

But not all campers were happy ones. I spoke with Judi Frazier Watson on June 10, 2020, and her recollection of Camp Chowenwaw was not nearly as pleasant as those of others. "The two most miserable weeks of my life I spent at Camp Chowenwaw!" At least that's what Judi had to say on the subject of summer camp. She admitted to being "a bit of a princess" and that "roughing it" for her now means spending time at a Holiday Inn. Still, she had many reasons to remember her time at camp with less than glowing terminology:

> *They made me eat stewed prunes. Can you imagine? At my house you had to try new things, but you were never forced to eat anything you didn't like. Not at Camp Chowenwaw! And I had to wash dishes, something I never had to do at home. And another thing—they had us sweeping the dirt in front of the Big Cabin where we ate most of our meals. I mean, I was a Class-A sweeper. I used to sweep up the front porch of my grandmother's house in Springfield as well as the sidewalk in front of her house, but I never knew you needed to sweep dirt.*

As if those things weren't bad enough, Judi objected to swimming in a pool with tadpoles swimming alongside her. That brought up another subject of contention. While she was gone, her family put in their own pool, and she was upset that she didn't get to see or to enjoy watching the construction of it. And the final proverbial straw came when she had as a cabin mate "the weirdo from hell" who awoke everyone in the middle of the night, swatting at bugs and spraying bug spray all over the place. Her whole experience was "awful and horrible!"

Sometimes when we look back, there is a glow and wonderful sensation that those days were so fantastic, but Judi reminded me that "all that glitters is not gold" and that summer camp could be as much an ordeal as a treasured memory.

When I spoke on the telephone with Pamela Chappell on July 16, 2020, she remembered Camp Chowenwaw as a great place. She recalled that there were chores to do every day, first at the individual campsites and then at the Big Cabin, where most meals were eaten communally. There were tables to clean and "Kapers" to perform in the kitchen, and she remembered with great fondness the flag raising ceremony performed every morning before breakfast. The ceremony was followed by the recitation of the Pledge of Allegiance and then the Girl Scout Promise.

Old, abandoned cabin at Camp Chowenwaw, 2020. *Author's collection*.

Campers on a nature walk at Camp Chowenwaw, twentieth century. *Courtesy of the Florida State Photographic Archives.*

There were, however, other memories—strange memories—that have stayed with her. She remembered the image of lines of white-capped swimmers tilting their heads to one side as the counselors would walk up to each girl and drop alcohol into her ear after a swim in the sand-bottomed pool. Then each girl would tilt her head in the other direction, and drops would be placed in the other ear. This was no doubt to help prevent swimmer's ear.

Another strange memory Pamela had concerned the rumor circulated that some of the counselors would open care packages from home and take the best "goodies" for themselves, but now that she is grown, she really doesn't think the counselors would do such things. Still, it is funny to think that such paranoia was rampant after a few days at camp.

Camp Chowenwaw is still a breathtakingly beautiful place, and that is due in part to the foresight of commissioners of Clay County who, in

Campers enjoying climbing one of many oak trees at Camp Chowenwaw, 1965. *Author's collection.*

2006, purchased the camp from the Girl Scouts of Gateway Council. According to the Camp Chowenwaw Park website, Clay County was assisted by the Florida Communities Trust using Florida Forever funds. Camp Chowenwaw is now open to the general public park, and it offers a variety of recreation, including "camping, events facilities, hiking, fishing, kayak access, volley ball courts, picnic areas, seasonal pool, Museum, nature center, and a playground."

The park is "now managed to preserve its historical and natural resources while offering recreational opportunities." Camp Chowenwaw was a "big sister" to all us "little sisters" for almost seventy-five camping years when it was "decommissioned on December 3, 2005." On that day, many grown women and probably some younger ones shed tears. Thankfully, this was only the beginning in a new chapter in the life of this place. The property has been saved and restored to new glory. Camp Chowenwaw Park will continue to serve as a recreational and camping area. For that reason and more, we *chowenwaws* can all be glad!

CAMP ECHOCKOTEE

(And Camp Francis Johnson/Camp Shands)

On my honor I will do my best—
To do my duty to God and my Country,
and to obey the Scout Law
To help other people at all times
To keep myself physically strong, mentally awake, and morally straight.

—The Scout Oath or Promise, Scout Field Book, *1948*

It was a damp day on October 5, 2020, when I drove to Orange Park to visit St. Johns River Base at Echockotee. This is the location of the Boy Scout summer camp Camp Echockotee, which many people of a "certain age" remember fondly. Presently, this camp is now half the size of its former configuration, and it serves as a day camp featuring aquatics—canoeing, sailing, swimming, and rowing. It also serves as a place for Boy Scout troops of the area to camp overnight during the year.

When I arrived, I met with Ranger Frank Geer. He pulled up in his pickup and kindly drove me all over the camp, which still has about eighty acres of land. We stopped first at Ashley Lodge, a beautiful dining hall that fronts the water of Doctor's Lake. The original building was hit by lightning in the early '90s and destroyed. The only part left standing was the fireplace. On September 25, 1997, a new building, with the old fireplace, was dedicated.

Ranger Geer and I continued our journey through the camp, and on our way to the next stop, we passed the pool and the forty-foot climbing/

View of Doctor's Lake from Ashley Lodge, 2020. *Author's collection.*

rappelling tower. Next, we passed the beautiful waterfront chapel, where several local weddings have been performed. We then passed the BB gun and archery ranges as we made our way past campsites with canvas tents and small fire pits. We also passed the Wood Badge Fire Ring, as the ranger called it.

The last place on the tour was the big Council Fire arena. A large open area contained a place where a huge bonfire could be built. In front of the stage, a wide stream of water flowed and separated it from a cement and aluminum gallery for big assemblies on the other side. A wooden walkway bridged the two areas, and Ranger Geer told me that Cub Scouts often ceremoniously "crossed over" to become Boy Scouts.

When I was searching for camp information in the Jacksonville Downtown Library, I came across numerous articles and photographs that helped me visualize the long-ago landscape of Camp Echockotee, as well as where boys of all ages could enjoy numerous outdoor activities. One item I found was an undated camping pamphlet, undoubtedly given to kids at Scout meetings before they arrived at camp. It was designed to help Scouts and their parents prepare for a week at camp. It was titled *Let's Go Camping!*

Camp Echockotee's camping booklet *Let's Go Camping!*, 1930s. *Author's collection.*

and prepared by the Greater Jacksonville Council, Boy Scouts of America. It was filled with all manner of information needed for the camping experience.

According to the booklet, Camp Echockotee was a Class "A"–rated scout camp by the National Council of the Boy Scouts of America. Its name came from a Native American term meaning "We are brothers." In this document, a brief history of the camp was included, beginning with its location. The 132-acre "reservation" was purchased in 1922 and located on the western bank of Doctor's Lake about two and a half miles southwest of Orange Park.

The first summer session was held in 1922, and at that time, there was only one permanent building on the property. By the time the pamphlet was published, there were twenty-one permanent buildings (By my count, the date of publication had to have been after 1937. It is also possible it may have been published much later, even into the '50s. It had no publishing date anywhere).

In addition to the buildings, the pamphlet said that there were "docks, boats, canoes, water tower, artesian well, baseball diamond, tennis court, electric lights, telephone service and other facilities for the health, safety and enjoyment of the campers."

During the first fifteen years of operation, the camp had over 8,733 boys attend one-week sessions, proving that the camp was very popular. The cost for each week was seven dollars per camper, with a fifty-cent nonrefundable registration fee.

There were so many things to consider in this pamphlet. Sections included such things as

> *What You'll Do at Camp*
> *Waterfront*
> *Handicraft*
> *Campfires*
> *Woodcraft*
> *Nature Trail and Den*
> *Sports and Games*
> *Equipment*

Several other sections offered a glimpse into a distant time. The section marked "Camp Regulations" didn't actually offer any regulations. It simply said:

> *A long list of rules and regulations is neither necessary nor desirable at Camp Echockotee where every camper is guided by the general provisions of the Scout Oath and Law. The boys are asked to observe only a few rules which are important to the safety and welfare of the entire group. Always under the guidance of capable, friendly leaders, the campers conduct themselves in the manner of well-bred Scouts and are glad to obey the few regulations established. It is very seldom that a camper cannot adjust himself to living in harmony with his fellows, but when this occurs, the directors are forced to send him home. In such cases, the camp fee cannot be returned.*

Another piece of interesting information talked about religious instruction. It was not to be neglected during the camping session. "THE TWELFTH SCOUT LAW" said:

> *A Scout is reverent and in the great outdoors created by the Almighty hand, every camper feels His presence. Sundays and weekdays are in keeping with this spirit. Grace is asked before each meal and ministers from Jacksonville and surrounding towns conduct a non-sectarian service each Sunday for Protestant campers. A lay worker is in charge of Jewish services and Catholic boys are taken to Mass at St. Mary's Home in Orange Park. Meals are arranged to meet religious customs.*

I found it touching that such noble ideals were all part of the camping tradition, and it is wonderful that this document still survives to evidence that fact. It is apparent that the goals of the camping experience of earlier generations were to instill basic concepts of character into countless boys who would grow into fine men.

One of my best sources for Camp Echockotee was C. Richard Leonard, who began Scouting and camping there in 1949. He eventually became an Eagle Scout, as did two of his sons and two of his grandsons. (This is probably some kind of record, but certainly not surprising.) Richard seemed proud of these accomplishments, and his devotion to Scouting was most evident.

We talked via telephone on October 7, 2020, and he told me that he considered camping at Camp Echockotee an "interesting venture." He

Keystone of the fireplace in Ashley Lodge at Camp Echockotee, 2020. *Author's collection.*

started camping on weekend trips with his Scout troop in 1949 and 1950. He started going to summer camp in 1951 or 1952. He went again in 1953, and by 1954 and 1955, he was part of the aquatics staff instructing campers in canoeing, rowing, sailing, swimming and water safety.

In 1990, Richard began his five-year tenure as an Echockotee Lodge advisor, and he was a member of the Order of the Arrow. Membership in this national Boy Scout fraternity/service organization is prestigious, since it identifies youth and adults who contribute greatly to Scouting.

I asked Richard what he remembered specifically about his time at camp, and he told me about three things. He was part of the aquatics staff, and every Saturday he had to clean the pool, built by Duval Coal Company. One Saturday, he slipped and hurt his back so badly that he could hardly walk. He made a walking stick for himself out of an oar from one of the canoes. To this day, his back gives him trouble because of that fall.

The second thing he told me was his memory of campfire activities, especially the one that took place on the first night of each camping session. He really loved the camaraderie exhibited when the boys sang camp songs—songs he remembered and was able to lead when he was called on to do so in the U.S. Navy.

The last memory Richard shared was of Cabin 13. From the name, I assumed that it was a haunted cabin, but I was wrong. Cabin 13 was a favorite with campers, he told me. It was two stories high, and it had a fireman's pole in it that started in the attic and went through the second floor, ending on the first floor. It was great fun to slide down fireman-style, and campers did so over and over again.

Patrick Hinely, my friend who had also been at Camp Blanding, also mentioned in his comprehensive email his experiences at Camp Echockotee. Patrick's Camp Echockotee experience occurred when he was a part of Boy Scout Troop 319, based in the parish house of the Lutheran church just south of Bolles School, across San Jose Boulevard from the San Jose Country Club's golf course.

A pavilion at Camp Echockotee, 1940. *Courtesy of the Florida State Photographic Archives.*

Patrick had a great story to tell about his Scoutmaster, Scott Comstock. To me, it sounded like Comstock was the quintessential Scout leader:

Scoutmaster Scott Comstock was a noble and patient man with a good sense of humor as well as a good working understanding of adolescent boy logic of the sort which sets in when the inevitable testosterone poisoning that goes with male teen years begins. As the decades have passed, Mr. Comstock strikes me as more and more remarkable. May he rest in peace. We never gave him much of that, despite which he cheerfully celebrated our successes and sang our praises, especially when parents came on visiting day.

What strikes me now as a funny event definitely did not seem funny at the time. Mr. Comstock had told us, before we headed to Orange Park, to leave our cigarettes at home, but being of that age when invincibility inspires stupid acts, several of us nevertheless brought along packs of smokes. I still don't know if someone ratted us out or if Mr. Comstock, himself a cigarette smoker (though also enough of an authority figure that we never challenged him on the kind of example he was setting for us in that regard) just happened to find us, or if he had figured it out. It was only the known smokers who were all simultaneously absent from the troop's camp site, and all he had to do was set out to patrol the periphery. In any case, he didn't have to go far to find us.

Every evening after dinner, we had a communal fire in the middle of our troop's campsite. That evening it burned even brighter than usual, at least for a few minutes, fueled by several packs of cigarettes, most still in their cellophane wrappers, going up in smoke, though none of us was smoking.

There is another source of information that I found invaluable when researching Camp Echockotee, but it came from an unlikely source. Nira Sue Trammell wrote an incredible book called *Front Porch Stories: Memories of Old Florida*, published in May 2019, not long after she died on April 30, 2019, at the age of eighty-seven. She was, by the way, able to see the manuscript before her passing, and I was assured by Lynne Raiser, her niece who went to the trouble to compile these stories and publish them, that Nira Sue was delighted with the product.

Campers at Camp Echockotee, 1940. *Courtesy of the Florida State Photographic Archives.*

In 1935, when Nira Sue was two years old, she and her family lived on the Camp Echockotee campgrounds. Her father and his assistants worked for the Wilson Cypress Company, and he was sent to build new cabins and restore old ones for the Scouts to use. As a matter of fact, he built the Pavilion that many campers remembered.

The Trammells lived on the property of the camp to allow the father to be better able to supervise his workers and to work himself. From 1935 to 1941, Camp Echockotee was the home of Nira Sue's family.

Nira Sue's book is a wonderful collection of her memories of her childhood at Camp Echockotee and later at Ortega Forest. She remembers many fascinating facts about childhood during the Depression while living on a campsite meant for boys. She told of how her sister Jane was chased by four wild boars into the swamp, where she had to tread snake-infested water until the boars lost interest in her and went away.

Nira Sue had a story about how the Scouts would often lock her in the icebox where the sides of beef were hung. She spoke of the rumors about pirates who used to come up a small creek to Wade's Spring just outside of the camp's front gate to bury their treasure. Sadly, she and her siblings found only arrowheads and blue and white beads left in the area by the Native Americans. She even had a story about Cabin 13, about how when she came down the pole one time, she landed hard at the bottom and her knee hit her head, breaking open her eyebrow. She didn't even go to a doctor to get stitches, which she probably needed.

There is one passage, however, that really sums up her experiences at Camp Echockotee, and it had to do with those pesky Boy Scouts. Nira Sue said:

> Jane [Nira Sue's sister] *and I considered the scouts that came on holidays throughout the winter and for the full summer camp season (1935–1941) to be a dreadful nuisance. They infringed on our privileges and curtailed our activities to a maddening degree.*
>
> *We were not allowed on the compound during the scouting season, nor could we play in the dam area or swim in the pool.*
>
> *We were allowed to attend the camp fires at the council ring, though, and had access, if we were careful not to be caught by a counselor, to Anna's kitchen. Between meals we could sneak into the Mess Hall, but we were not supposed to have any contact with the scouts at all. But we did. The scouts sought us out.*
>
> *In spite of the rules, Jane held sway as the local environmental expert and was often consulted as to the layout of the camp by newcomers. I was just a tagalong. But we knew where all the fun things to do were located.*

After reading her wonderful book, I concluded that the Little Rascals of the early cinema could not have lived better adventures than Nira Sue and her siblings!

There are many people who contributed greatly to Camp Echockotee and the Boy Scouts, but there is one man who really stood out and, for me, became a real mystery. Francis Johnson was a most interesting character. His family owned the Dinsmore Dairy, and he and his sister were heirs to a great fortune. But Francis Johnson died penniless, since he and his sister gave all their fortune away before they died. Many people who went to Camp Echockotee remember this man because he built and ran the woodshop and taught woodworking to campers.

When Francis Johnson wasn't working at the camp, he was often seen riding his bicycle through Jacksonville. He would even ride his bike from downtown to Hope Haven Hospital to show movies to the sick children there.

My friend Patrick had this story to tell about Francis Johnson:

> It was summer 1965 when I went, along with about a dozen others from Troop 319, for a week at Camp Echockotee, over in Orange Park, which was then the back of beyond.
>
> At that age, fire held enough of a fascination for me that when I encountered a pile of smoldering wood shavings outside a small building in the woods, I tried to fan them into flames, until being gently but firmly dissuaded from doing so by a little old man with white hair who said thank you but that the shavings burned at just the right rate all on their own and ought to be left alone.
>
> He introduced himself as Mr. Johnson. That building, the wood-turning shop, with several lathes, was his domain. Inside, several of my fellow scouts were merrily creating more wood shavings by pressing chisels into pieces of spinning wood. After he thought I'd observed long enough, he put a chisel in my hand and turned me loose. I made a lamp which has proven quite durable. Fifty-five years later, it still works. It sits on my bedside table.

This Mr. Johnson is also the person who donated land for a camp built very near to Camp Echockotee. However, information about Camp Francis Johnson has been hard to find. Camp Francis Johnson was across Kingsley Avenue from Camp Echockotee, about five miles away, and it has since been replaced with a residential subdivision. I could not find any information about when the camp was formed or why it was developed so close to another Boy Scout camp.

It has been suggested to me that the camp was originally formed so that African American Boy Scouts could also enjoy camping—Scouts in the South were segregated until the '60s. Francis Johnson was the sort of person who wanted everyone to have the opportunity to camp. There is no written documentation, though, to prove any of this.

What does exist is information in the Jacksonville Downtown Library's vertical files that begin in the 1970s after desegregation laws were enacted. The first article ran in the *Florida Times-Union* on June 30, 1974. The headline said, "Rotary Activity Area Dedicated at Scout's Camp Johnson." The article went on to say:

> *The Rotary Club recently gave $15,000 to the council* [North Florida Council of the Boy Scouts of America] *to remodel an existing swimming pool and to add a chlorination facility, chain link fence, program shelter and new restrooms to adjoin the Rotary Activity building contributed several years ago at the camp 2 miles south of Orange Park High School.*

The next article was published on June 13, 1975, in the *Florida Times-Union* about "Cub Scouts Shooting BBs" and taking gun safety classes at Camp Francis Johnson. Then, about two years later, on August 17, 1977, an article written by Woody Russell ran in the *Jacksonville Journal*. It was titled "Camp Francis Johnson—Sale of Scout Property Eyed," and it quoted North Florida Boy Scout Council's Simon Smith as saying, "The board of directors adopted a long range plan in November [1976] which recommended the camp be sold, that the organization consolidate 'our efforts' and find other property farther away."

Apparently, it had become clear that Orange Park's population was encroaching on the camps of Camp Echockotee and Camp Francis Johnson. There were stories told of campers being able to hear the nearby traffic and even the sound of radios from nearby houses. So, the Boy Scouts made plans to sell the two-hundred-acre property of Camp Francis Johnson—the nearby camp.

The council was asking $1 million or $5,000 per acre for the Camp Francis Johnson land. Smith went on to say, "We do need space for growth and use, but we need to have it better spaced for the availability of the members."

On May 1, 1978, a *Jacksonville Journal* article announced, "Clay Camp Site Sold"—175 acres of Camp Francis Johnson had been sold to Marvin Wilhite, a developer, for $875,000. Wilhite's plan was to build a subdivision, and the Scouts would be allowed to use the property until the developer had need of the land.

Above: Color Guard resting by the river at Camp Echockotee, 1982. *Courtesy of the* Florida Times-Union.

Left: The fireplace in Ashley Lodge at Camp Echockotee that had survived a lightning strike fire and was included in the renovations, 2020. *Author's collection*.

At this point, the trail of information about Camp Francis Johnson came to an end. On January 27, 2021, I spoke on the telephone with Robert Burns, North Florida Council facilities director of the Boy Scouts. He told me that there is no clear path of ownership to verify exactly how the money from Camp Francis Johnson was used, and he had no information to verify that the camp was originally built for African American Scouts.

While all of this was happening, Camp Echockotee continued with business as usual. One article, "Days to Remember For Ex-Boy Scouts," was written by Ray Knight, and it ran on July 6, 1973, in the *Jacksonville Journal*. From this article I found a great deal about the fireplace of the dining hall/activity center.

Knight said that the original fireplace had been built in 1948 using the stones sent by other Scout troops throughout the United States, and it was a feature story covered in *Scouting Magazine*. Thankfully, the fireplace survived the lightning strike in the '90s and could be incorporated into the new building dedicated in 1997.

It is quite interesting how the fireplace was originally constructed. Knight's article quoted Ben Edwards, the director of support services for the North Florida Boy Scout Council, as saying, "To build the fireplace originally, they [local Scouts] wrote to scouting groups all over the country and asked them each to send a rock from their area."

From that call for rocks, Camp Echockotee received 633 stones, pebbles and other mementos. These included:

> *A tomahawk from South Dakota…A pebble from Francis Scott Key's birthplace…Marble from Mount Rushmore…A rock from Kit Carson's home in New Mexico…Another from Mark Twain's studio in Elmira, N.Y…One from the vicinity of Henry Ford's home at Dearborn, Mich…Gold ore from Ontario…Rock from the home of Patrick Henry at Martinsville, Va…And others from the birthplace of Wilbur Wright at New Castle, Ind.: Pike's Peak, Colo.; and Valley Forge, Pa.*

The next year, on July 14, 1974, the *Florida Times-Union* covered the second annual "Echockotee Days to Remember," and Jesse-Lynne Kerr wrote an article titled "Days to Be Recalled Next Week." She was able to interview Circuit Court judge Harold R. Clark, who was serving as chairman for that celebration. He told her:

The fireplace in Ashley Lodge when new, 1949. *Courtesy of the Florida State Photographic Archives.*

What I remember most [about Camp Echockotee] *were the swimming periods in the pond, in the lake, and the cold showers in the morning under the dam spillway. Then there were the hours spent paddling the Indian war canoe across and up the river, camping over night in an orange grove somewhere near Fruit Cove and going on to Green Cove Springs and back.*

But for real excitement and sometimes sheer terror, I remember the capture-the-flag games. I always hoped to be on the team with the biggest toughest guys, but most of the time I'd find myself in a patrol to drive off the enemy getting too close to the flag. I was determined to stay alive (Keep my armband from being broken) but most of the time I became a casualty sooner or later.

Probably the most poignant of all the articles I found appeared in the *Florida Times-Union* on August 14, 1982. It was titled "Boy's Special Gift Waves in Dad's Honor," and it was written by Stephen W. Holland. He told the story of Jimmy Mims, an Orange Park Cub Scout, who donated to Camp Echockotee the flag that had draped his father's coffin.

Gloria Suder Mims, Jimmy's mother, noted that of her three children, Jimmy (who was only five when his father died), had suffered the most because of his father's passing. She said, "It is so hard for him because he cannot remember his father. He didn't have the memories the other two had. Their father did a lot [with them] because they were older."

According to the article, Jimmy had originally wanted to give the flag to his Cub Scout troop, but Betty Neikirk, director of the Black Creek Day Camp, was able to convince him that Camp Echockotee could really use a new flag. Jimmy was thrilled at the suggestion, and with the blessing of his other siblings, he began the process to give the flag to the camp.

Then, on August 13, 1982, Jimmy and his mother were at the raising of the flag at Camp Echockotee as one hundred Scouts looked on. Gloria Mims said that when she asked Jimmy how he felt, he said, "Daddy has the best seat in the house."

The Boy Scouts of Northeast Florida still operates three camp properties: Camp Francis, Camp Shands and St. Johns River Base at Echockotee. The Boy Scout camp called Camp Francis may or may not refer to Francis Johnson. According to its website, Camp Francis is owned by the "Camp Francis Trust and is set aside for usage by the North Florida Council BSA." This camp also "features several wooded campsites, a large open field, a shelter at the old house site, pit latrines and city water. The site is perfect for advancement work with new Scouts or for troop games in a private setting."

Camp Shands is in Melrose, and according to the website of The Order of the Arrow—Echockotee Lodge 200, it was in the 1960s that the Baden Powell Scout Reservation was purchased. Thomas Baker and his business associate William Shands, who was a candidate for Florida governor, were instrumental in acquiring the land. The Meninak Club of Jacksonville

Flag-raising ceremony at Camp Echockotee, 1982. The flag that had once draped the coffin of the father of Scout Jimmy Mims rises over one hundred Scouts at Camp Echockotee. *Courtesy of the* Florida Times-Union.

Will Courtney learning to sail at Camp Echockotee, 1993. *Courtesy of the* Florida Times-Union.

provided a lodge with limited cooking facilities, storage and a trading post. Then, in 1967, the camp opened for its first summer session. It would be the 1980s before any amenities were available. The Taylor Dining Hall was built in 1980–81, and platforms for tents were available at that time as well.

The Camp Echockotee of earlier times is now called St. Johns River Base at Echockotee. It may be a bit smaller in size than the camp earlier generations knew, but it still has a beautiful campus and is a wonderful place to enjoy the outdoors and water activities. According to the St. Johns River Base at Echockotee website, the base has "8 large campsites, a dining hall, meeting rooms, plus many pavilions" for Scouts of all ages. It is "open for individual and troop camping from September through April every year. Aquatics Camp opens May through August."

As our world has changed around us, Camp Echockotee has had to change. Thankfully, it retains much of its original splendor—towering trees, thick green underbrush and a commanding waterfront on Doctor's Lake. This is a setting where young men can develop skills as they enjoy camping traditions passed down from Scouts long since grown. As I stood in the center of the camp, trying to imagine generations of boys who had been there, I could easily understand why Camp Echockotee is a favorite for so many grown men of the northeast Florida region.

CAMPING CULTURE

Gear

Before I began this chapter, I purchased a reprint of a book written in 1877. The author was John M. Gould, and his book was titled *How to Camp Out*. I figured that with such a title and such an old text, I should learn a great deal about how people of an earlier time approached living outdoors. I was immediately drawn into Gould's book when he acknowledged in the first chapter the following:

> *The hope of camping out that comes over one in early spring, the laying of plans and the arranging of details, is, I sometimes think, even more enjoyable than the reality itself. As there is pleasure in this, let me advise you to give a practical turn to your anticipation.*

Even in those long-forgotten times, a time long before the idea of Boy Scouts was a flash in Baden Powell's brain, Gould knew that anticipation is important in the lives of humans. His next paragraph shows that things have certainly changed. He told the reader to:

> *think over and decide whether you will walk, go horseback, sail, camp out in one place, or what you will do; then learn all you can of the route you propose to go over, or the ground where you intend to camp for the season. If you think of moving through or camping in places unknown to you, it is important to learn whether you can buy provisions and get lodging along your route.*

I would hope that this book was intended for adults or older children. Even the thought of little kids getting ready to camp in this way sends chills through my mother's heart. It does show, however, that camping in the nineteenth century was far more rigorous than it was in subsequent times. There were fewer "civilized" campsites with places cleared for tents or fires, and cabins would have been a luxury.

In a chapter titled "Getting Ready," Gould included a long list of items, after which he warned, "Be careful not to be led astray by it into overloading yourself, or filling your camp with useless luggage. Be sure to remember this."

He did not seem to follow his own advice. His list had 114 items, and I am certain he was using a wagon for transporting it all. (He did include a half barrel of axle grease). His list included cooking utensils like a Dutch oven, stove, frying pan, coffee pot and shingles (for plates). There were foodstuffs like figs, bacon, salt, pork, fish, coffee, molasses, mustard, sugar and tea. A toothbrush was also included.

As I read through all of Gould's preparations and recommendations, I realized that nineteenth-century camping meant something far more primitive than most of us have ever known. His book was intended to be used by seasoned adventurers who were headed out into wilderness. Camps, as we know them, were in the future.

By the 1930s, when Camp Echockotee put out a short manual called *Let's Go Camping!*, there was an actual place that had been prepared for Scouts to go—Camp Echockotee. This place had many more amenities than Gould's campers would have known. There were pavilions where Scouts could gather, and there were cabins and platforms for tents to be pitched where Scouts would sleep. There were places for fires and a mess hall where most meals were eaten communally.

In this Camp Echockotee booklet, there was a section titled "What to Bring to Camp." For me, reading this list of supplies provided me a poignant glimpse into the past. Life in the '30s was still more rustic than it is today or even when I was a kid in the '50s and '60s. Scouts were to bring these things with them to camp:

2 or more blankets
Mosquito net
1 regulation uniform (shorts recommended)
1 pair of pajamas or "nightie"
2 suits of underwear

2 or 3 pairs of shorts
Bathing suit
1 pair of tennis or canvas shoes
1 pair of heavy shoes
Towel
Soap
Toothbrush and paste
Comb
Raincoat or poncho
Scout knife and hatchet
Bible
New Testament or Prayer book
Boy Scout Manual
Notebook and pencils
Letter paper and envelopes

The need for mosquito netting was very telling. Florida campsites near any body of water certainly swarm with the unwelcome pests in the summer, so this item is understandable. The Boy Scout knife and hatchet were certainly needed to do crafts and to clear underbrush or to chop kindling. One of the most surprising notions was that a camper would need only "2 suits of underwear."

Naturally, there were no electronic devices, since they were years in the future, but I was surprised that there was no listing for a flashlight. Perhaps they might have been too expensive for most people to allow their sons to take them into the woods.

I was touched that there was need of Bibles and prayer books. Church going was more prevalent in those days, I would imagine, and religion was not to be neglected. I also found it heartwarming that the boys were to write home and keep their parents apprised of their activities.

By the time the '80s rolled around, the list of necessary supplies was a bit different. In the *Florida Times-Union*, there was an article titled "How to Prepare for Camp," written by Wini Rider and published on May 29, 1980. It discussed all sorts of things a potential camper might need to know. Toward the end of the article, there was a list of things campers would need to take on their summer camping experiences. Campers would need:

Sleeping bag plus one extra blanket.
All-weather jacket with pockets and hood.

Heavy sweater.
Sweat suit or sweat shirt, if he has one.
2 pairs of shorts.
Jeans.
T-shirts.
2 bathing suits, preferably the fast-drying kind.
Underwear.
2 pairs of pajamas.
Hiking boots.
Rubber soled shoes (gym, jogging or deck shoes.)
6–8 pairs of socks.
Baseball hat or crew hat to serve as sun hat.
Bandana that can be used as a sweat band.
Small pillow or cushion covered with dark material.
Comb, toothbrush, toothpaste and soap.
Knife, fork, spoon (Don't buy those clever knife, fork and spoon sets that are assembled like a jackknife. Try cutting your meat with your fork at the end of your knife.)
Plastic plates and plastic thermal cups for hikes. (Don't buy mess kits. Hot food on tin plates are too hot to hold on laps.)
Small knapsack for hikes.
Fabric laundry bag.
Three towels.
Facial tissue.
Flashlight. Buy a disposable flashlight which is an all-in-one battery unit for the young camper. He will either lose it or it will be ready to be thrown away by the time camp is over. And don't forget batteries for the big camper's flashlight.
Plain khaki-colored rubber ground sheet to be put under sleeping bags. (Instead of a ground sheet, your camper can take an old shower curtain or one of the large plastic mats which are sold everywhere.)
Rain slicker or poncho. Remember that a poncho is almost impossible to swim in. So, it is not recommended for wear while boating or canoeing.

According to the article, all of these items were to be put into a large duffel bag, a nylon sports bag, a large backpack or a large laundry bag—not a suitcase or plastic garbage bag.

More than fifty years after Gould's book was written, the Camp Echockotee manual was published in the early '30s. Another fifty years

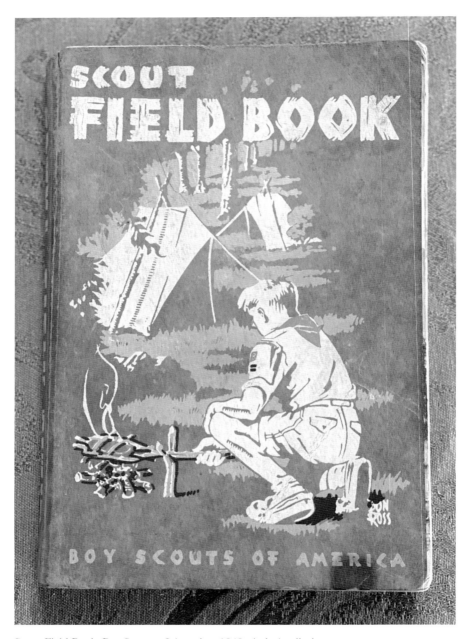

Scout Field Book: Boy Scouts of America, 1948. *Author's collection.*

passed before the *Times-Union* offered its article on how to prepare for camp in 1980. Each source reflected the differences in camping gear from one period to the next and, in doing so, reflected how lifestyles and sensibilities had slowly changed.

There is one other book I wanted to mention before I ended this chapter. It is titled *Scout Field Book*, written by James E. West and William Hillcourt and published in 1948. I couldn't resist getting this book. I ordered it online, and within a few weeks, it arrived from Pepper's Old Books in Hanson, Kentucky. This awesome book is still a treasure-trove of pictures and information on a host of activities that goes along with the camping experience. It was divided into seven sections:

> *It's Fun to Be a Scout*
> *Hiking Along*
> *Camp Crafts*
> *Wild Life*
> *Helping Others*
> *You*
> *Our America*

Not only were there two pages of equipment for personal use and for patrol needs (pages 138 and 139), but this book also included information about how to set a broken leg and how to rescue a drowning Scout. It had information about how to pitch a tent, how to tie knots and how to crack a whip. In the "Wild Life" section, there were pictures of all manner of mammals, reptiles, insects and birds that a Scout might encounter, and in my copy, there were pencil checkmarks on the tops of most of the drawings. This led me to believe the owner of this book had actually seen each marked critter.

On page 28, there was a form to be filled out by the owner of the book. From the faded penciled-in blanks, I learned that the owner of the book was in Troop 108 in Jackson, Kentucky; that Mr. Wireman was his troop leader; and that they had their meetings on Mondays at 6:30 p.m. Nowhere could I find the name of the Scout who wrote that information, and that made me a little sad. I can just imagine this unnamed young man at his desk one night in the late '40s as he dutifully filled in this information. Nowhere else could I find any other personal information about this kid. I did find, between pages 106 and 107, an old, delicate oak leaf pressed near the spine, and again, I wondered about the person who put it there.

After all my research, interviews and readings, I think Mr. Gould was only partially right about camping—that anticipation may be an important part of the experience, but revisiting our camping experiences can also be "even more enjoyable than the reality itself." It doesn't matter if the experiences are mine or not. There is a universal joy I can experience as I think about preparing to camp, as I think about actually camping and then as I think about how the experience unfolded. There can be little doubt that those of us who have experienced the beauty of northeast Florida in its wilder states have been and were made better for all of the area's camping realities.

GOLD HEAD BRANCH
STATE PARK

(Later Called Mike Roess Gold Head Branch State Park)

I am the first to admit that Mike Roess Gold Head Branch State Park is not a summer camp. Sure, a person can go camping there in the summer. They can go camping there all year-round. They don't even have to be part of a group, but I wanted to include this camp in my book for two reasons. The first is I heard it mentioned quite frequently when I was a kid. I had friends who went there with their families, and they all seemed to have had a good time. Second, it caught my eye as I made several journeys to other camps in the area, and it looked so inviting each time I passed by it.

I consulted my grade school best friend, Margo Dovi Feichmeir, because she was one of those who had been to Gold Head with her family. She emailed me back on October 1, 2020, to share what she knew about Gold Head State Park:

> *Gold Head had houses for rent back in the day, and my family did this a few times, once with several families, in the off-season (I believe fall) and on the weekend. I didn't realize it was a camp. I remember it had woodsy walking trails with an historical marker about the inventor of the cotton gin, and a large (to a child) lake for swimming. That is about it.*

According to an email I received from Alex Cronin of the Florida Department of Environmental Protection's Press Office, Gold Head State Branch Park officially opened on April 15, 1939. With the growing affordability of automobiles during the late 1920s and early 1930s and the

Left: Entrance sign for Mike Roess Gold Head Branch State Park, 2020. *Author's collection*.

Below: The gate of what is now called the Mike Roess Gold Head Branch State Park, 2020. *Author's collection*.

increasing popularity of Florida as a vacation destination, parks such as Gold Head Branch became a desirable destination for local residents and out-of-town visitors.

Presently, the camp is called Mike Roess Gold Head Branch State Park, and it is located less than an hour outside of Gainesville and about an hour's drive from Jacksonville. This park contains one of the few remaining examples of an old-growth stand of longleaf pines in Florida. Alex said that the park has

> the rolling sandhills of the Florida's North Central Ridge, which spans Highlands, Polk, Osceola, Orange and Lake Counties. Marshes, lakes and scrub provide habitat for a wide variety of wildlife within the park. A steephead ravine with seepage springs forms Gold Head Branch and bisects the park. Most stream valleys develop through gully erosion caused when surface water carries sediments off the top of the group. Steepheads, however, are formed differently. Ground water leaks upward through porous sand onto a sloping surface. In doing so, the water removes sand from the bottom of the slope, causing the sand above to slump down and be carried away by the stream. Steephead ravines are continuously lengthened as the seeping water erodes them from the bottom up.

She went on to say that Gold Head Branch is one of Florida's first state parks. In 1935, it became part of the Florida state park system. Martin J. "Mike" Roess donated the initial property that was then developed by the Civilian Conservation Corps into a park. In 1933, during the Great Depression, Franklin D. Roosevelt launched the CCC to put the unemployed workers to work. Cronin said that the park was known as Gold Head Branch until 1966, when the Florida Board of Parks and Historical Monuments changed the name to honor the late Mike Roess.

She added,

> In Florida, CCC enrollees were instrumental in developing the first eight parks in the Florida Park Service. From 1933 to 1942, the CCC and the Works Progress Administration (WPA) programs constructed an impressive collection of facilities throughout the state. Gold Head Branch State Park was one of those original eight parks, and many of the CCC buildings are still standing and welcoming visitors more than 70 years later. In 1935, 25 seasoned craftsmen from Company 2444 were sent to the Gold Head site, where they were joined by hundreds of CCC youth and established Camp SP-5.

Picnic pavilion at Mike Roess Gold Head Branch State Park, 2020. *Author's collection.*

Stone wall probably constructed by the CCC at Mike Roess Gold Head Branch State Park, 2020. *Author's collection.*

When I drove through Gold Head Branch State Park, I could easily make out those buildings made by the CCC. Those buildings have a lot of stonework, and they are usually marked. There were some stone retention walls that I suspect were CCC handiwork as well. The entry gate to the park is a great example of that work. It was one of the first of the CCC buildings.

Alex said that even today, eighty years after the park's opening, visitors can still use any of nine rustic cabins facing Lake Johnson. They can also prepare for a swim in the old bathhouse.

CAMP IMMOKALEE

Within the breast of nature throbs the heart of God.
—motto for Camp Immokalee

On August 21, 2020, I had a telephone interview with a man named Cal Marshall, who contacted me about helping with this book. Cal was just six years old when his association with Camp Immokalee began in 1950. For the next seventy years, he was in some form or fashion part of Camp Immokalee as a camper, a staff member, an assistant director, a director or a supporter of the camp and all that it offers. Even after he came back from his tour of duty in Vietnam, he spent several summers working at the camp to help himself reintegrate into nonmilitary life. As he put it when we were winding up the interview, "Camp Immokalee is a magical place, and I have a great fondness for it."

Cal told me that the camp opened in 1909. He said that the 120-acre camp appealed mostly to those who were into rustic camping, until right after World War I. Camp Blanding needed to use some of the property to accommodate many soldiers returning to the United States, so the place became a canvas tent camp for those veterans. Because many were fearful that this was not the last world war and Camp Blanding might need to expand, one-third of the Immokalee property was taken by the U.S. Army through eminent domain. Today, Camp Immokalee boasts about 86 acres.

Cal said that Reverend Edwin F. Montgomery (of Presbyterian Camp Montgomery fame, a camp just a few miles south of Camp Immokalee, and one that would be formed years later) was instrumental in helping Camp

Totem pole of Camp Immokalee with Cal Thomas and other staff on top, 1959. *Courtesy of Cal Thomas.*

Camping Staff at Camp Immokalee with Cal Thomas in third row, fifth person from the left, 1966. *Courtesy of Cal Thomas.*

Immokalee become a residential camp. Montgomery procured CCC workers to come and build ten wooden cabins in a semicircular configuration, some of which still remain as renovations of their originals. Montgomery went on to create his own camp for the Suwannee Presbytery, and the owners of Immokalee were able then to sell the camp to the YMCA after World War II.

According to Cal, during the time between the First and Second World Wars, the Jacksonville YMCA was raising money to build a complex downtown complete with dormitories and swimming pool. Sadly, just about the time of the stock market crash in 1929, the head of the YMCA, who managed the fundraising monies, supposedly ran off with all the cash and went to South America. The building dreams were left in ruin and camp projects in limbo. But the winds of fortune changed. With the help of two high school service clubs—High Y Clubs for boys and Y Teens Clubs for girls—Otis B. Hennet, a missionary and charismatic organizer, was able to get the camp idea going again.

According to Cal, Hennet began looking for the most talented High Y and Y Teen members to fill positions at Camp Immokalee. He would invite them to serve in leadership positions at the camp. In that way he was able to have the best and brightest staff, and that meant that campers were more likely to return for subsequent summers, keeping the coffers

Campers at a young Camp Immokalee, 1925. *Courtesy Jim Austin.*

filled because of the high quality of instruction in a variety of activities. There were many things that filled campers' days—archery, riflery, nature lore, Native American lore, pioneering forest crafts, boating, canoeing, swimming, horseback riding and gymnastics.

Rumor had it that campers were often able to find Native American arrowheads and pottery shards after rainstorms near the shoulder of the roads in the camp. These "findings" led to the assumption that Native Americans probably summered in the camp's location in earlier times. There is also the name itself. *Immokalee* is Mikasuki for "your home."

Cal also supplied me with a comprehensive schedule for a normal day at camp, and it is no wonder campers probably fell into a deep sleep at the end of a day. The schedule of a normal day was:

> *A bugle would play Reveille.*
> *There was a morning skinny dip in the lake.*
> *A Bible reading took place while campers were still in towels.*
> *Campers would then get dressed.*
> *The KP (Kitchen Patrol) was called to prepare breakfast as each cabin's remaining members cleaned up and around the living quarters.*
> *Roll call would take place after campers assembled.*

There was then a flag raising ceremony.
Announcements followed.
Next, breakfast was served.
A work period would follow—campers would take care of areas of erosion
as well as pick up trash around the camp.
There was a Chapel service.
Activity #1
Activity #2
Before lunch there was a swim in lake until KPs are called.
Lunch was served.
There was a one-hour rest period.
Activity #3
Activity #4
Everyone was allowed an afternoon swim in the lake before supper.
KPs were called to prepare supper while campers dressed.
Then followed the flag lowering ceremony.
Supper was served.
Organized games were next—baseball, volleyball or nature hike.
An evening program took place in the chapel. There were skits, singing and
ghost stories.
There was a clean-up time.
Taps was played on a bugle.
Finally, it was time to turn out the lights.
Every night after "lights out," a counselor would come in each cabin and
say a little homily about how to live life with the values of cooperation.

Cal went on to say that on the last night of each camping session, there would be an Award Ceremony. One year, Cal had the honor of being chosen as the Honor Camper, a camper chosen by his camp mates. Needless to say, this was a very great and meaningful award for Cal, and its impact has had a lasting effect on him.

I spoke with another longtime Camp Immokalee participant, Jim Austin, who came to my house with an armload of Camp Immokalee memorabilia. He told me that his connection with the camp could be traced back to 1918, when his grandfather returned from World War I. Jim's grandfather had no hope of getting work in Blackshear, Georgia, his hometown, so he went to Jacksonville to seek his fortune. Unfortunately, at that time, the city was experiencing an influenza epidemic, so he headed south of the city to a place called Keystone Heights.

Campers in long boats at Camp Immokalee. This picture was titled "Harry and his Crew," and nearby pictures in the scrapbook were dated 1925. *Courtesy of Jim Austin.*

Jim told me that the property on which Camp Immokalee stands had been an encampment first for soldiers returning from the Spanish-American War and then for veterans of World War I. Eventually, the encampment would be a place where ordinary citizens could come, and for a nickel a night, they could stay in one of the tents.

There were two pieces of information for which I had been searching. One was about whether or not Neil Armstrong had ever been a camper at Camp Immokalee and the other was about the missing totem pole.

Jim told me that on the property there still stands a cabin called the Eagle Cabin. It is presently used by the staff only and is in need of many repairs. Rumor had it that on the July night the Apollo Eagle Lander touched down on the moon back in the summer of 1969, the boys in this cabin renamed their quarters "Eagle Cabin" in honor of America's great space achievement.

Jim says the cabin probably had always been called the Eagle Cabin because that was where the leaders traditionally stayed, and the name was usually reserved for leaders. He did say, however, that somewhere inside, near the door of that cabin and high in the rafters, there is a signature that says "Neil Armstrong." Now, whether it belongs to the first man to walk

Eagle Cabin, where famous signatures can be found, 2020. *Author's collection.*

on the moon would be a matter of conjecture and impossible to prove. Still, it is interesting that all of these "rumors" seem to circulate about this particular cabin.

I was also curious about the magnificent totem pole that once graced the property back in the day. Austin told me that in the late '40s, the Foley Lumber Company that was located on Main Street in Jacksonville, Florida, had a shipment of lumber coming in from the Pacific Northwest. The owner purchased two authentic Native American totem poles and had them brought into Jacksonville with his order of lumber. One pole was erected in front of his store on Main Street, and the other he gave to Camp Immokalee. The fate of the totem pole at the lumber company is unknown. I have searched for photos and advertisements, but I could find nothing.

The totem pole at Camp Immokalee became too rotted away to safely allow it to stand, so it was taken down. Allison West, the present-day camp administrator, said that a smaller totem pole replaced the original for a number of years, but it too had rotted away. It was eventually blown over in a storm, she told me, leaving a small indention in the foliage where it had once stood.

Jim Austin was also most generous with all of his Camp Immokalee memorabilia. He was one of the lucky campers who had found at least two magnificently preserved arrowheads on the Camp Immokalee property, and he allowed me to photograph them and hold them in my hands. He also provided me badges and certificates along with histories and photographs dating back into the '30s. Unfortunately, most of the photographs were too small to be placed in this book; they were copies of originals that were scattered to unknown locations. No matter, I was thrilled to be allowed to see and to touch these things. It almost breathed life back into the times long gone.

One interesting story came to me from Steve Baranek, the son of Ranger Hal, an iconic 1950s and '60s television personality on a local children's television show. I spoke with Steve on the phone on June 15, 2020, and he related to me his ill-fated camping experience with his family at Camp Immokalee. The whole family had gone together, and they stayed in a large cabin there. His father was there to support the Boys Clubs of America as part of his job. Steve wasn't wild about going. He would have rather stayed at the neighborhood swimming pool than go to a camp far away.

As luck would have it, the rains arrived just as the Baraneks did, and it didn't let up until they left. It was an awful time. One of the Baranek children got sick with an earache, and the family finally gave up and left earlier than planned. Steve thinks he might have been the one who was sick.

Rick Peacock, another camper to contact me, told me in a telephone interview on June 1, 2020, that he got to go to Camp Immokalee sometime in the early '60s, maybe around 1962. Rick got to go to camp for two weeks at his grandmother's expense. This tradition would continue for many summers after. Camp Immokalee was his favorite camp, and he remembers that there were no bad events. It certainly was a happy place for him.

He had three interesting and amusing memories. The first explained why the campers had to wear shoes. As was customary, the kids would take their meals in the biggest and one of the oldest buildings on the property, the Mess Hall. It was wooden, and it was surrounded by a layer of pine straw that the kids lined up on as they filed into the hall.

Arrowhead found at Camp Immokalee, 2020. *Courtesy of Jim Austin.*

Before each meal, the headmaster would ring a bell (a ship's bell that was sold in 1975 for some strange reason) and then make announcements before grace. One day, the head councilor rang the bell, and when he had the attention of the campers, he said that this day would have a show-and-tell portion. He put a big sack on the table, and from that sack he pulled a huge, dead coral snake.

"This snake was recovered from just outside where you all were coming in to eat. Your shoes actually trampled this snake because he was hiding under the pine straw you all were walking on. If you had not had shoes on, he could have bitten anyone of you in the bare foot! This is why we insist that you campers wear shoes at all times when you are outdoors, even when you are on the way to the lake to swim!" The room got very quiet.

Another story Rick related was that one afternoon, the boys were forced inside their cabins because of a thunderstorm. These were big wooden cabins with rafters and bunk beds. As they waited for the rain to stop, one of his friends encouraged him to come high up into the rafters and sign his name with all the other campers who had signed before. When Rickie got up there, he couldn't find any space where he could sign his name. Suddenly, his buddy said, "Here's a T. Peacock. Could that be your dad's signature?" It was! Up there with all the countless other names of generations of campers.

It is interesting to note that many other famous locals left their mark on the walls of Camp Immokalee cabins when they were campers as kids. According to a *Florida Times-Union* article written by R. Michael Anderson titled "Summer Camp Memories" that ran on July 26, 1995, there were signatures of former mayors Jake Godbold and Lou Ritter, former senator Ander Crenshaw, Clay County sheriff Dalton Bray, Jacksonville city planner Ray Newton, former assistant superintendent of Duval County Schools Bobby Knight and attorneys Charlie Towers, Doug Milne and George Gabel Jr.

Rick Peacock's last story occurred when he finally got home from a two-week camping session. His mother was supervising the unpacking of his suitcase when she happened to notice that the bar of soap she had packed for him had hardly been used. "The DIAL hasn't even worn off, Rickie," she fussed at him. "Why have you used so little of your soap?"

He replied, "Well, Mom, we were in the lake swimming every day!" Rickie was all boy!

Another camper who had a story to tell was Tom Burrows. We spoke via telephone on July 15, 2020. He told me that back around 1952, he had the

A wall of signatures, 1994. *Courtesy of the* Florida Times-Union.

good fortune to meet a kid named Jerry Alderman who encouraged him to volunteer at the Downtown YMCA. (Jerry Alderman would grow up to be a theoretical and particle physicist. He earned a doctorate and had numerous accomplishments in many fields of endeavor.)

As a result of those hours serving as a volunteer, Tom was able to become part of the kitchen staff at Camp Immokalee the next summer. That meant that he was not only paid a small stipend for his work in the kitchen, but he also received free access to the camp activities. "It was a great way to spend summer!"

By his second year, when he was about fourteen, Tom had been promoted to being Director Hennet's assistant in classes like the Snake Lore class, where he got to handle snakes. Students even had the opportunity to eat rattlesnake steaks. Tom went on to teach swimming lessons, and he got to determine who belonged in which ability level— Minnow, Fish or Life Guard.

He got to share the same quarters with all the other staff members. "It was a laugh a minute in that place. We kids liked to pick on each other and carry on like kids do. It was great fun!"

Renovated cabins at Camp Immokalee, 2020. *Author's collection.*

Construction on Ranch Immokalee, 1991. *Courtesy of the* Florida Times-Union.

He recalled one outstanding memory that might have given parents pause. A big school bus had come to take them deep into the woods, and when the doors of the bus opened, there was a dead rattlesnake, although no one knew it was dead at the time. It had been coiled up and its head propped up with a stick so it looked like it was about to strike. Fun times!

Still, Tom relished his time spent at Camp Immokalee. "It was awesome to make friends with all the guys I spent time with. Those were friendships that lasted all through our youth. I was blessed to be able to be part of this. And when it was time to go back to school and all that, I felt awkward in long pants—no longer in shorts and swim trunks that we wore all summer long."

He wishes he could put his hands on one, but there is a promotional brochure somewhere out there that bears his photograph on the front. "They said mine was an All-American image that would represent Camp Immokalee very well. I don't know about all that, but it certainly showed me to be a very happy kid! Like I said—going to Camp Immokalee was a great way to spend a summer!"

I spoke with another camper, Thomas Smith. We talked on the phone on May 7, 2020, and he said his best camping experiences came when he went to Camp Immokalee. Every morning he was awakened by a bugle, which made him think of the army. They had to walk everywhere in a kind of march, and they were always lining up for something. There was a PX type of store on the property where he discovered Grapette soda and Zero candy bars, and these became his go-to snacks. Campers could accrue good behavior tickets to buy such treats.

He was able to go horseback riding, but he seemed to have enjoyed canoeing more. As a matter of fact, he still goes canoeing today. He spoke with considerable animation about his happy time camping, and Camp Immokalee seemed to be his favorite.

The mention of horseback riding reminded me that on May 14, 1994, an article written by Anne Sponholtz ran in the *Florida Times-Union* on that very subject. According to the article, Camp Immokalee was going to reinstate horseback riding activities into its summer programs after a twenty-five-year absence. "Ranch Immokalee" came into being when the YMCA—with many volunteers—built a beautiful facility that still exists today.

The article was about the dedication of Ranch Immokalee, a facility located across the road from the main portion of the camp. The dedication had taken place on May 5, 1994, and the article said:

Ranch Immokalee, 2020. *Author's collection.*

Campers will feel as though they have stepped into the old West. A dark, wooden fence complete with two white wagon wheels marks the entrance to the stables. An old fashioned hay wagon sits at the stable entrance, which is decorated with window boxes filled with flowering plants. Twelve stalls will soon be the homes of the horses who will be making Camp Immokalee their summer quarters.

The article went on to say that Jerry Martin, district vice president of the YMCA, reported that the horses had been "carefully chosen and donated" because they had to be "gentle and good with kids."

Do not think that Camp Immokalee was just for boys. Before the '80s, boys' camp and girls' camp ran at different times. Then, in the early '80s, cabins were added that were for the exclusive use of the girls, and boys used the older cabins. My classmate and friend Ellen Shanks Rosenblum spoke to me on May 19, 2020, all about her exploits at Camp Immokalee. She told me that she comes from a family of camp people. She, her husband, her son and even her mother in the mid-1930s went to numerous camps all over the United States.

One of several horses that campers can ride at Camp Immokalee, 2020. *Author's collection.*

When Ellen was eleven or twelve in the early '60s, she went to Camp Immokalee. "I had a real coming-of-age experience at Camp Immokalee. When I was there when I about eleven, I was put into a cabin with thirteen-year-olds. A few of these cabin mates were bullies to me and were relentless with their badgering. Fortunately, these mean girls were reported—not by me, by the way—I think by the other cabin mates who took pity on me, and suddenly, I was okay. That was until they told me that I had to tell them everything I knew about the Birds-and-the-Bees. It was sort of like, we'll take you in, only if you can tell us. Fortunately, I had a friend whose older sister had told me all about such things, so I made my presentation and was off limits after that!"

Another of her Camp Immokalee memories came when it was time to put on skits or talent shows in the open-air social hall. She and her friends April, Amy and Diane were going to be the Beatles and lip-sync one of the band's songs. Much to their disappointment, their skit was rejected by the staff, and they had to come up with something else. So they became the Dave Clark Five instead, as if that were a less racy choice. She surmised that the girls had decided not to run their new act past the organizers. Better to beg forgiveness than get permission. Needless to say, they were a big hit!

Lesley Ketchum Deaver talked to me about her time at Camp Immokalee on August 1, 2020, when we spoke on the phone. Lesley is presently a middle school teacher in Fernandina, and she has some very fond memories of Camp Immokalee. She said that she doesn't remember all that much about childhood events, but her days spent at Camp Immokalee, starting in the summer of 1990, really stand out in her mind.

> *I went there for several summers in a row for a week or so each session. And I really loved it. I remember one thing that really stands out and that was getting to go tubing in the Lake Bradford. We campers would wait our turns on the dock. It was so exciting! But one time I got thrown off the tube, and I remember being terrified as I waited for the boat to return to pick me up. I tread water for the longest time just praying that nothing was in there with me. We all were afraid there were gators in the lake!*

One of the fortunate things that Lesley's mother did was to save several of Lesley's letters home from the time she was away at Camp Immokalee. Her mother had taken her to the store weeks before camp to buy pretty stationery for letter writing. Even now the colors of these letters are vibrant and the wording is absolutely charming—complete with misspelled words and all.

Lesley wrote to her parents in one *Garfield*-designed note:

> *The food is grose (But don't worry I'm not going to starve. We haft to eat it.) We haft to got to bed at 10:30. By the way if you want to wright me you can. Got to go now!*
> *Love, Lesley*
> *P.S. I really miss and love you.*

Another letter talked of her schedule, which she spelled "scugule." She was up at 7:15 a.m., then they raised the flag. Next was breakfast, followed by swimming lessons, drama and then tubing. This was all before lunch. They then had a rest period back in their cabins where Lesley would write her letters and eat snacks. In the afternoon, she went to dance, then hydro-sliding, and before dinner, she and the others went canoeing. She ended her account by saying, "This place is so fun!"

When Lesley first showed these letters to me, she apologized profusely for all her misspelled words, but I reminded her that a little girl just did not carry a dictionary to camp. I actually admired her ability to sound out the words she wanted to use. These are indeed precious keepsakes.

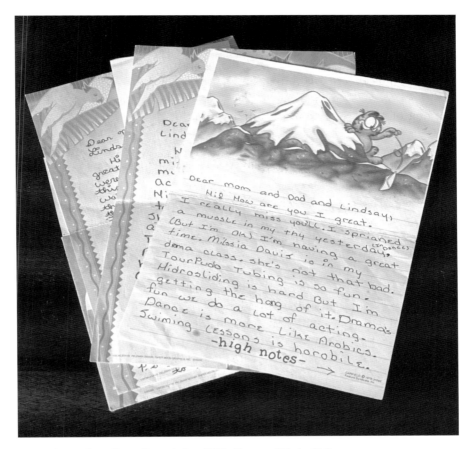

Letters home from Camp Immokalee, 2020. *Courtesy of Lesley K. Deaver.*

There were other memories Lesley recalled. "It's odd what you remember. There was a snack machine nearby, and during the rest period, I loved getting something out of it to eat. So weird."

She also remembered that they usually held a dance at the end of the week just before they all went home. She added that by the end of the session she and her cabin mates would have developed crushes on some of the guys, but the kids mostly ended up just standing around all night as the music played.

Now that she is grown and has some perspective on life, she concluded our interview with the assertion, "Camp Immokalee was really a blast!" And if her little girl epistles are any indication of her feelings for the place, we can all be assured that, "This place is so fun!"

I had a phone interview with Tina Basney Biggers on June 11, 2020, and when Tina began telling me about her time as a junior counselor at the Jessie Ball duPont YMCA Day Camp, I listened to how she and the other counselors really loved their time working with children. As a matter of fact, Tina realized that she wanted to work with children when she grew up because of her experiences as a counselor. Today, she is a teacher of pre-kindergarteners at Westview Elementary School.

But what really seemed to make her come alive was when she told me about her time as an Indian Princess at Camp Immokalee when she was much younger. The Indian Princess organization, sponsored by the YMCA, was designed to get fathers and daughters together to spend quality time with one another. (Indian Guides was an organization that the YMCA sponsored that got fathers and sons together.)

Tina had some special memories of her time spent in Indian Princesses. She remembers that she, her father and her big sister were in the Shoshoni

Indian Princess crafts and ceremonial object (Camp Immokalee), 2020. *Courtesy Tina B. Biggers and Beth B. Seeker.*

Swimming race in Lake Bradford at Camp Immokalee, 1960s. *Courtesy of Cal Thomas.*

Tribe. Her father, Bill, was the chief. Beth and Tina named him Big Eagle. His daughter Beth became Little Eagle, and Tina became Eagle Feather.

Tina recalled a ceremony when they were camping at Camp Immokalee during which the chief, carrying a torch, would arrive from across the water in a canoe. This torch was to be passed to the eldest daughter in a literal "passing the torch" ceremony. During this particular special moment, the torch Big Eagle carried fell on his eldest daughter and burned her on the arm. She bravely endured the pain of the burn, but she still carries a scar.

Both girls loved the Indian Princess tribe and camping out at Camp Immokalee with their father. Their mother still has a box of their projects made during some of these special times. They include a tomahawk, many patches, feathers, necklaces and two renderings of eagles—one big and the other little.

My own daughter Mandy was an Indian Princess with her father. She named my husband, Hardy, "Blue Dove," and the other fathers like Grizzly Bear and Mountain Lion gave him no end of grief, as I recall. But he endured their teasing because he and his Little Dove spent many fun evenings camping and being together in the woods at Camp Immokalee.

Camp Immokalee is a place of countless treasured memories for many men and women of this area, and it continues to provide wonderful memorable activities for those who camp there. The summer of 2020 didn't have a full campground because of the pandemic. About half of the normal camping population attended, and by all indications, summer camp was still a success.

Of all the camps I researched for this project, Camp Immokalee seemed to be one of the most popular—the one most mentioned by friends and colleagues. Its influence on the lives of so many people is immeasurable, and my hope is that Camp Immokalee can continue far into the future.

CAMP KEYSTONE

*A*fter many attempts to locate this camp, I accidentally came across it when I got lost looking for a different camp. I had been told there had been a camp run by the Salvation Army somewhere near Orange Park. I had also located some photographs of kids in attendance at a Salvation Army camp in the Florida State Photographic Archives. These pictures were listed as being in Jacksonville. So, on the day as I headed to Camp Montgomery to do an interview, I wasn't expecting to find Camp Keystone.

All of a sudden, a sign appeared at the end of what I thought was a dead end. It said, "The Salvation Army Camp Keystone." I stopped my car and quickly made a note to get in touch with the director there. Then, I hurried on to get to my other interview.

When I arrived home, I began my search for information on a camp that I almost wasn't going to include in this book. What a mistake that would have been!

A cool, breezy day greeted me on November 18, 2020, as I made my way back toward Starke, Florida, to Camp Keystone. There I met with Monica Reifer, guest services director of Camp Keystone and Conference Center. She was warm and hospitable, and first, she provided me with a brief written history of the camp called "Keystone Camp and Conference Center Fast Facts."

Lessons at Salvation Army Camp (possibly Camp Keystone), 1953. *Courtesy of the Florida State Photographic Archives.*

This document said that the Salvation Army Lake Bradford procured eighty acres of land on Lake Bradford in 1916, from an estate. (Presently the camp has about three hundred acres.) The site was given to the Salvation Army with the understanding that the land would be developed into a camping area. Sadly, World War I and the Great Depression disrupted American lives so much that making the camp a reality was not going to be easy. It certainly wasn't going to happen quickly, either.

According to the history, it wasn't until the 1944 that Brigadier Ernest Pickering, Salvation Army of Florida divisional commander, "inspected the

Weigh in at Salvation Army Camp (possibly Camp Keystone), 1953. *Courtesy of the Florida State Photographic Archives.*

land and decided the property would be used for under-privileged mothers, children and for Salvation Army youth."

By contacting Camp Blanding, the Salvation Army secured three buildings built by the CCC, and in 1945, Camp Keystone began accepting campers. In modern times, more than two thousand children attend summer camp at Camp Keystone each year, except for 2020, of course.

As Monica drove me over the compound in a golf cart, she told me that the property opened as a "fresh air" camp, a place where underprivileged city kids could go to enjoy nature. Since 1946, the camp has had sessions for many children to enjoy. It was primarily designed to help poorer, malnourished children get three good and healthy meals every day and enjoy a wholesome environment.

The website said:

> *Many children from low-income families rarely experience life outside their immediate neighborhood. That's why The Salvation Army's annual summer camp programs are so important. Every year, thousands of kids get a fresh perspective on life as they meet new friends, discover new activities, and get a taste of the great outdoors. As campers learn to swim, play sports, create music, make art, and scout, their trained counselors help them navigate the complicated emotions and struggles often associated with their lives back home.*

The camp I saw was amazing, and I would think little kids from the city would be awestruck with the size and beauty of the Camp Keystone's layout. Along with an Olympic-sized pool and large Worship and Activities Center, Conference Center and Dining Hall, there were multiple complexes with rooms for overnight stays—Keystone Inn, Keystone Lodge, Keystone Cabins and Keystone Hotel. They had the Highrope Challenge Course for team-building activities, a stable with horses to ride and several outdoor assembly areas, including one near Crystal Lake. There is even an old chapel brought from Camp Blanding right at the gate to remind campers immediately of God's presence in this place, just in case the beautiful trees and rolling hills wouldn't do it.

Some amazing facts were included in the history of the camp. It employs 115 seasonal employees with 24 permanent staff, which includes groundskeeper and manager. There are 543 beds on the property, and on any given day, 800 people (campers and people attending conferences) can be on the campus. They can prepare as many as 1,200 meals each day or 115,000 pounds of food throughout the entire summer. Over 1,000 s'mores are consumed each season (only 10 campfires a year), and it is, as the history says "One life changing experience."

On May 7, 2020, I spoke with Thomas Smith on the telephone about the Salvation Army camp he attended quite a while ago. He told me he thought it was located near Orange Park. (As far as Monica knows, Camp Keystone was the only Salvation Army camp in the northeast Florida area. She said that Camp Keystone actually serves the entire state of Florida.)

Mess Hall at Camp Keystone, 2020. *Author's collection.*

Left: Window in the chapel at Camp Keystone, 2020. *Author's collection*.

Below: Barn for the horses of Camp Keystone, 2020. *Author's collection*.

Highrope Challenge Course at Camp Keystone, 2020. *Author's collection.*

Thomas said that his mother was divorced, and he got to go to camp while she worked at State Farm. He thought he went as a day camper. The whole experience contained a great deal of religion, he remembers. He didn't mind, though. They held chapel every morning and had Bible story lessons each day. He also recalled that after each swim, alcohol was put in each camper's ears as a precaution against swimmer's ear. He has very

Chapel at the gate of Camp Keystone which was moved from Camp Blanding, 2020. *Author's collection*.

Outdoor chapel/gathering place near Crystal Lake at Camp Keystone, 2020. *Author's collection*.

warm feelings about his experience there, although no one event seems to stand out.

On the day I visited Camp Keystone, I enjoyed the cool breeze that swept through the sunny oaks and bright happy buildings. I couldn't help but feel the nurturing quality of this remarkable place and the people keeping it going for underprivileged kids who need enrichment and care. I suppose it actually pays to get lost every once in a while. You never know what treasures you might find.

CAMPING CULTURE

Food

I know an excellent writer who lives in Monroe, Louisiana, who has the greatest titles for her books. Shellie Rushing Tomlinson has written many inspirational books and has her own podcasts running on the internet; she is best known for her humor. When her cookbook came out, I rushed to buy a copy of *Hungry Is a Mighty Fine Sauce*, and I laughed all the way through it. I couldn't help but think that this title is so accurate. When a person is hungry, almost anything can taste good. And that has to be especially true for kids staying at summer camp. "Hungry" is indeed the sauce that makes camp food palatable.

The institutional nature of the food served in the dining halls of camps could be overlooked after a kid has spent four hours swimming, two hours hiking to and fro to activities and three hours doing chores that needed doing. Add to that letter writing and playing pranks on one another, and it is quite probable that most kids at camp would be ravenous at each meal, despite its taste, smell and texture. Well, maybe not at first, but as the days dragged on, all things began to taste pretty good.

It was also certain that there would be mishaps cooking around the campfires—the blackened-to-a-crisp hot dogs, the underdone, gritty potatoes in the foil-pouch stew, the ignited and blackened marshmallows that topped the s'mores. Campers would eat these things anyway, especially after having trekked miles to set up camp. It didn't matter that the supper was raw or unrecognizable.

I thought it was important to consult camping guides on this matter of food to really get an idea of how things worked in camp kitchens and at campfires.

I found two excellent books to help leaders provide nutrition to campers. The first is titled *Kettles and Campfires: The Girl Scout Camp and Trail Cookbook*. This was a Kessinger's Legacy Reprints of the book written in 1928. At that time, culinary tastes were strikingly different from our palates today.

This book has two sections. The first is called "In Camp" cooking. It was all about nutrition, the economics of buying food in bulk and the preparing of meals for large groups. There was a chapter on planning menus, one on how to set the tables, one on how to safely store the food and one on following sanitary standards for the health of all campers and to avoid contagion and food poisoning.

"On the Trail" cooking had to take into account all provisions that needed to be transported, sometimes miles, on the backs of campers and in canoes. Bulky foodstuffs were to be avoided, and each item needed to be carefully packed—like eggs wrapped in newspaper and placed carefully in the coffee pot. The list of items could be stowed into five small duffle bags and one knapsack, and they would weigh 120 pounds all together. The four-day, ten-girl canoe and camping trip had almost two full pages of food items to feed everyone. It included such items as sardines, prunes, nuts, peanut butter, oatmeal, canned fruits and vegetables, eggs and bacon.

There were recipes for things like biscuits, corn bread, cereals, chowders and stews, eggs and cheese, potatoes and cheese and meat and fish dishes. The desserts included fruit fritters, marguerites, gingerbread and applesauce.

I would think that there are very few local girls who have been on a four-day canoe trip with all their knapsacks each filled with twelve pounds of food items. Most of the cooking experiences of north Florida campers were probably for one or two campfire meals. They were probably more like Cindy Mathiesen's favorite memory—the canoe breakfast. Once a week at her sessions at Camp Chowenwaw, she participated in this breakfast ritual, and as she told me about it, I could tell by the sound of her voice that it really meant a great deal to her.

Early in the morning on the appointed day, we girls would arrive at the Big Cabin and collect small, single-serve cereal boxes, small cartons of milk, and bananas. These things were put into milk crates, and we would then troop down to the basin where we would board our canoes. We would then paddle down past the Jungle Trail, around the bend, to Peter's Creek which was just off of Black Creek. We had a special shore where we usually tied up, and here we would eat, while we watched the sunrise.

I suppose one of the wonders of camping is how one can collect a treasure of memories that encapsulate rare times in one's life—like sunrises over a creek in Florida or the taste of Cheerios and bananas when you are hungry.

The second cookbook I read was lent to me by my friend Claire Fleming King. This cookbook is titled *Cooking Out-Of-Doors*, published by the Girl Scouts of the U.S.A. in 1960. It was a far more colorful book than *Kettles and Campfires*, but it still covered many of the same things. *Cooking Out-Of-Doors* had colorful dividers that were marked with the title of the section. These sections were

> *Fireless Foods*
> *Kettle and Skillet*
> *Toasting, Broiling, Planking*
> *Baking*
> *A Whole in a Hole*
> *Ember Cooking*
> *Gimmicks and Gadgets*
> *Edible Wild Foods*

"Fireless Foods" were mostly salads. "Kettle and Skillet" had stew recipes, chili recipes and some bread recipes. "Toasting, Broiling, Planking" had meat recipes as well as a variety of recipes that could be made with toast. "Baking" recipes required a reflector oven, and the section included recipes for breads and muffins. "A Whole in a Hole" had recipes that used a Dutch oven, buried in a hole that would then have a fire built on top of it. "Ember Cooking" had recipes that were put into individual cans to be placed on the embers of a fire for a certain amount of time.

In the next-to-the-last chapter, "Gimmicks and Gadgets," there were instructions on how to build the ubiquitous Buddy Burner along with instructions on how to cook on rocks or with sticks. As for the last chapter, "Edible Wild Foods," the one on eating what is offered by nature, well, I would not ever try any of these foods. I would be certain to poison myself. I wouldn't be able to differentiate black (sweet) birch from *Gaultheria procumbens*. Still, I am glad that they included this chapter. It reminded me to avoid forest food before earning a merit badge in wild horticulture.

I think that eating at camp was mostly all about staying alive and less about taste. That doesn't mean that we didn't grumble about the food. No cafeteria anywhere is safe from the cruel comments of kids. Take it from me. I was a teacher, and what I would consider very good to eat, kids would turn up their noses at it. It just isn't cool to like the food you are given to eat when you are young. Like stewed prunes, maybe. Still, I love that so much care and attention was paid to these activities—the cooking over a fire and passing down the traditions of weenie roasts and such. I am thankful that there are still summer camps and campsites that honor these culinary delights made better by a sauce called "hungry."

CAMP MONTGOMERY

I have great memories of Camp Montgomery, because I have been there often—as a kid and as an adult. It is a lovely place near Starke, Florida, with about 167 acres of land and 2 to 3 lakes—Emerald Lake, Big Crystal Lake and Little Crystal Lake (When the water table is high, there is only Crystal Lake, since big and little lakes spill into each other).

I went to Camp Montgomery one summer, and I have been there on numerous youth retreats and other church-sponsored activities. Always, I have an immediate happy feeling when I think about Camp Montgomery, and I certainly felt that way when I went there to interview Zach Leopold, director of operations, on August 11, 2020. As the foliage began to overarch my car as I drove from the highway to the office, I was filled with a youthful enthusiasm and buoyancy reminiscent of a young camper.

Zach allowed me to roam about and take pictures of the grounds. I also was allowed to take photos inside the main office, and I got to meet some campers who were on the grounds. The lovely day really did take me back in time.

One prominently displayed newspaper article hung on the wall. It was titled "'Mr. Mont' is the father of camping," and it was written by Larry Humes and published in the *Florida Times-Union*. (The date had been cut off the clipping, but 1981 was written on the copy). Camp Montgomery became a reality because of the efforts of a distinguished Presbyterian minister—Reverend Edwin F. Montgomery.

According to the article, Reverend Montgomery was born in North Texas, and he had lived there throughout his youth. He got into camping

One of the cabins at Camp Montgomery, 2020. *Author's collection.*

when he worked as a camp counselor in Oklahoma, while he was in college. For two summers, starting in 1913, he worked at a YMCA Camp. The camp was located in an area rumored to have served as a hideout for Jesse James. It was called the "Devil's Den." Montgomery often said that he considered those summers working with both boys and girls as a "tremendous experience."

In 1915, he graduated from Princeton with two degrees in divinity. He received a call to McIntosh, Florida, where he served as a minister for a Presbyterian church there. During the summers, he would run makeshift camps at various locations for the boys of the church. When World War I broke out, Montgomery went into chaplain training to help with the war effort, but the war ended before he could complete his training.

He then went to Scotland on a two-year fellowship, and when he finished, he was called to Jacksonville to serve as minister to the Westminster Presbyterian Church. Five years later, he went to Lake City, where he served in the Presbyterian Church there for forty years. During the early part of his ministries, he became interested in providing camping experiences for kids in the northeast Florida area.

Above: A photograph of Reverend Montgomery when he was a counselor at Camp Immokalee, long before he established the camp that bears his name. *Courtesy of Jim Austin.*

Opposite: Certificate verifying that Shands Commander had completed various projects at Camp Immockalee, 1932. Reverend Montgomery's signature is on it. *Courtesy of Jim Austin.*

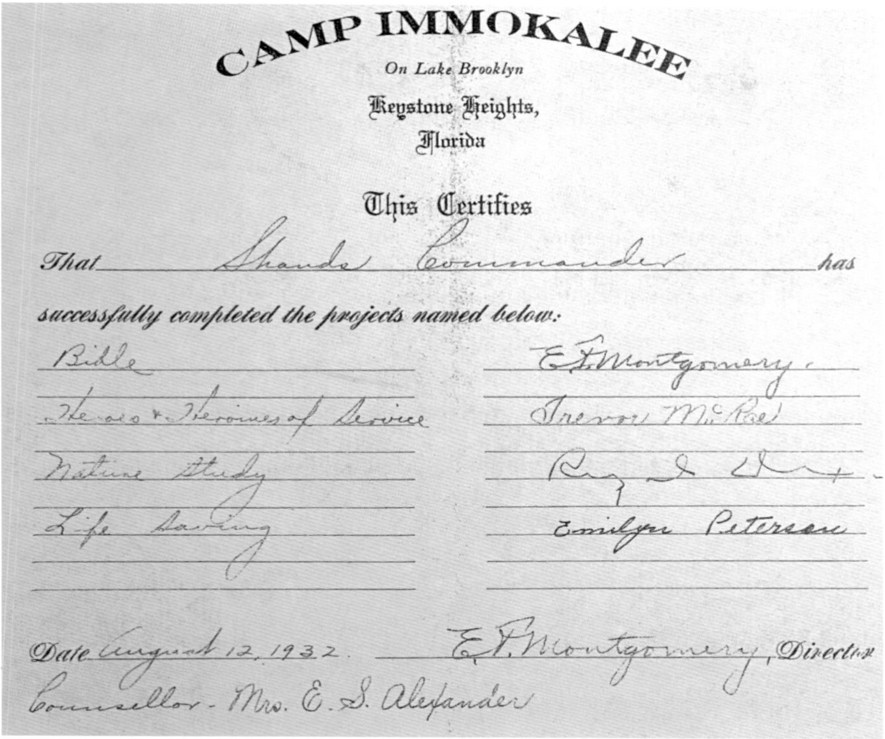

CAMP IMMOKALEE

On Lake Brooklyn

Keystone Heights,
Florida

This Certifies

That _____Shands Commander_____ has

successfully completed the projects named below:

Bible	E.F. Montgomery
Heroes & Heroines of Service	Trevor McRae
Nature Study	Ray S. Dt
Life Saving	Emilyn Peterson

Date August 12, 1932.   E.F. Montgomery, Director

Counsellor- Mrs. E.S. Alexander

According to the article, Montgomery was the assistant director of Camp Echockotee near Doctor's Lake. Later, he helped organize the YMCA's "Camp Immokallee [*sic*]" and helped operate it. In 1932, he helped create O'Leno State Park and was even instrumental in arranging for the Civilian Conservation Corps to come and build new facilities at the camp. For many years, he rented part of the property for his Christian Youth Camps, and he charged campers ten dollars for ten days. For twenty-five years, his camps were very popular. He constantly needed more space. He even conducted summer camps on his own property bordering the Suwannee River.

IN THE MID-1950s, MONTGOMERY lobbied the Suwannee Presbytery to purchase 160 acres of wooded area along Lake Crystal and Lake Emerald, and in 1957, the camp officially opened. They named it for Montgomery and his "pioneering efforts and contribution to youth camping."

When he was in his eighties, Reverend Montgomery was still active at the camp that bore his name. He might have been hard of hearing, but he still assisted at the camp by teaching a few crafts or leading some of the religious activities. He said:

> *What we've tried to do with our camps is make them enjoyable while, at the same time, teach the boys and girls about Christianity and about life. We try to give them responsibility. Over the years, we have had some youngsters who have had trouble at home. For many, camp made a difference; they have gone home changed and with a different outlook on things.*

On May 7, 2020, Mae Hotchkiss Johnson and I talked on the phone about her memories of Camp Montgomery, and one memory she shared occurred when she was a youth group counselor at Palms Presbyterian Church. She had taken a group of kids to Camp Montgomery, and since she loved to fish, she thought that she would bring her rods and reels to try her hand at fishing in one of the lakes on the campus. She would, of course, have to do her fishing before the kids awoke, since swimming activities were certain to scare away the fish. Still, she was determined to try her luck at it.

She stopped at a ramshackle bait shop along the way and was incredulous to learn that the bait one uses in these parts was worms. She was more of an ocean fisher, but she bought a container of worms just the same, and the next morning, she set out before the sky lightened or the kids were up so that she could catch a few fish. She said:

> *It was simply amazing watching as Emerald Lake woke up. There was a thin layer of fog above the water, and the color of the water lived up to its name. It was magical as the sun rose and I fished from the dock. Within the first thirty to forty minutes I had caught sixteen fish. It was amazing. Sadly, I couldn't convince the camp cook to prepare them for breakfast. Some of the fish were pretty tiny. Still, it was a great memory!*

Brad Rush shared one of his memories of Camp Montgomery when we spoke on the phone on June 17, 2020. It is one of Brad's most enduring memories of Camp Montgomery, and it came on the last night when his group had to put on a skit at the final performance of the camp session in Eppert Pavilion. He had to sing a solo of "Jeremiah Was a Bullfrog" and wear as good a costume as he could make from available supplies, which weren't very plentiful.

He also recalled a person at Camp Montgomery named David "Fearless" Fike. Brad and his young camping buddies looked up to this fifteen-to-

Right: Eppert Pavillion at Camp Montgomery, 2020. *Author's collection*.

Below: Camp Montgomery's Lake Emerald, 2020. *Author's collection*.

sixteen-year-old who was the coolest guy ever. Apparently, Fearless Fike feared nothing, and that brought to Brad's mind a variety of episodes so scary, I suppose, that he would not discuss them. Even so, he and his associates all had a kind of hero worship going on there.

Brad loved Camp Montgomery and called his times there as "foundational," as they provided him with many of his core beliefs. He had started going there with his friends from Lakewood before he turned ten. Later, he would take day trips there with South Jacksonville Presbyterian Church when his family changed churches. He loved the canoeing and swimming and picnics. Brad is eternally grateful for his times at Camp Montgomery.

Jennifer N. Redman told me on May 21, 2020, when we talked on the phone that she remembers fondly going to Camp Montgomery for multiple weeks each summer between the ages of eight and eleven. She enjoyed all sorts of activities that were offered there: swimming in the lake, learning how to sail, kayaking, canoeing and even boating to learn how to water ski. She is a self-admitted arts and crafts lover, and she was particularly fond of the skits and plays each cabin would put on in the assembly area outside.

She wasn't Presbyterian. She was a Baptist, but her family privately booked her space through a family friend who babysat for the family. This friend eventually became a camp counselor and even met her husband at Camp

Campers from Lakewood Presbyterian Church assembling for a hike at Camp Montgomery, 1966. *Author's collection.*

Montgomery. The only drawback that Jennifer could recall was the summer when she was stung by a caterpillar. Apparently, there were caterpillars all over the camp that year. Bummer!

I spoke with yet another Camp Montgomery camper, Pamela Chappell, in a telephone interview on July 16, 2020. She told me she enjoyed camping all of her youth and primarily went camping with her church group. She said:

> *I remember that Reverend Benz* [senior pastor at Lakewood Presbyterian Church] *would often accompany us on some of our retreats. We would all pile in our cars and go there, and the overall sensation of camping there, as I recall, is that it was hot, sticky, and sandy. Unlike other camps with their green trees, Camp Montgomery was hotter because its trees were more scrub oaks, and the camp was not as thickly forested.*

She also remembered that there were always skits to be enacted in Eppert Pavilion on the campus and sunrise church services were special memories for her. Despite the heat and sandiness, the whole time spent at Camp Montgomery proved "relaxing" and "uplifting." Pamela loved swimming out to the platform in the middle of the Crystal Lake, and she recalled that campers loved to run down the hill to the water and whatever swimming activity going on there. Going back up the hill proved quite a chore, however, and that was particularly true during one memorable incident when a heroic senior guy carried an injured female swimmer all the way up the hill to get her first aid. That kid was ever so "gallant," and many of the girls practiced a little "hero worship" after all the dust settled.

One aspect that I haven't really addressed yet is co-ed camping and how the counselors dealt with the call of "the birds and the bees." This certainly had to be a concern for camps with co-ed populations.

When I was at Camp Montgomery for my interview, I was introduced to Tommy Lane, who is now the CRE (Commissioned Ruling Elder) at McIntosh Presbyterian Church in McIntosh, Florida, and who is also the president of the board of present-day Camp Montgomery. He told me when he was a young camper at Montgomery, there were a lot of "wonderful kisses" to be stolen out there in the woods. As a matter of fact, he told me that he was one of the happiest of kissers. What with all the fresh air and hormones flowing freely—it seems only natural that infatuations were certain to have happened. Thankfully, they discovered that the secret to camp harmony was to keep everyone busy so only very chaste exchanges ever occurred—as far as he knew.

Tree canopy at Camp Montgomery, 2020. *Author's collection*.

There is one story in Camp Montgomery lore that tells of a more permanent pairing. On July 7, 2013, an article written by Claire Reed ran in the *Florida Times-Union* about Laura Beard and Nathan Renstrom. This story, titled "Summer Camp Was Just the Start," is also proudly displayed in the lobby of the present-day camp.

Camping staff of Camp Montgomery, 1995. *Courtesy of Camp Montgomery.*

The article said that these two Jacksonville natives had attended Camp Montgomery as kids. They had even found pictures in the archives that show them only a few feet apart, but they never got to really meet each other until 2005, when they were both counselors at the camp. By 2007, they found that they were drawn to each other, despite being very different. Laura was a former Miss University of Florida who would eventually earn a law degree from the University of Florida and was working to pass the Florida Bar at the time the article was written. Nathan was described more as a dirt bike rider who attended University of Central Florida. Their times at Camp Montgomery eventually led to more serious feelings and proved to them "just how summer romances can form over s'mores and sing-alongs."

It wasn't easy for them to hide the fact that they were dating, something their boss discouraged but didn't forbid. They were to keep it quiet when they were with the campers, but kids always know. Laura and Nathan weren't fooling anyone that they cared for each other.

When they weren't at Camp Montgomery, they continued their romance long-distance—she at UF and he at UCF—and as the years passed, their affections grew deeper. On May 18, 2013, Laura and Nathan were married at Palms Presbyterian Church in Jacksonville, and that was that.

Handprints of Camp Montgomery campers, 2020. *Author's collection.*

I am certain Reverend Montgomery would be happy that the camp that bears his name still carries on, despite the numerous obstacles that arise—like Covid-19 and the ever-difficult financial issues with which all camps must deal. I suspect that Montgomery is carefully checking up on the place even now. As the sun sparkled on the lakes and the trees bowed in the breeze, I could almost make out his footsteps.

CAMP SEMINOLE

This camp proved a bit of a mystery, and I had difficulty pinning it down. It seems that this camp was a day camp that operated in Orange Park/Clay County for a small span of summers, and it was run by a number of very enterprising Duval County School administrators and high school football coaches. I still haven't found anything written about it, but I couldn't leave it out since so many people had memories of it.

The first person I talked to was Chuck E. Sewell. We spoke on May 7, 2020, in a telephone interview, and he told me that he is a proud member of the class of '64 at Lee High School and a retired advertising sales manager. In his youth, he worked his way through many sections of the *Florida Times-Union* since his grandfather Bruce Goodloe was a legendary journalist there.

Chuck told me how much he enjoyed going to Camp Seminole, located in Orange Park on Doctor's Inlet, adjacent to Camp Echockotee. Every summer day, he would take a bus to the camp and join about two hundred other boys and girls in a profusion of activities. The children would break off into tribes with Native American names. Then, the groups would circulate through activities such as fishing or boxing or swimming in a sand-bottomed, freshwater, spring-fed swimming pool surrounded with wood plank docking. They had arts and crafts, archery, a rifle range, bunk houses for weekend campers and pavilions where they were served PB&J sandwiches for lunch. And all these kids were most certainly drowsy on the bus ride home.

According to Chuck, the place was run by several legends of the educational community—Warren Kirkham, principal at Lee; Virgil Dingman, head coach at Lee; Nolan Dingman, his brother and one of the bus drivers; Bob Lockett, who was principal at Jackson; and Welcome Share, who also was an educator. Running this camp placed these men in good positions to see their present and future students in a positive and fun environment. Here they could "bond" with kids in a noneducational environment so that when school started, the children would be less likely to misbehave.

One event really stood out to Sewell. "There were two guys who were in my age group who had won blue ribbons in boxing. I could tell that one was really not as good as I was, but when we were in a match, this kid had a left hook that came out of nowhere which knocked me out of the ring, not once, but three times."

Still, Sewell talked a great deal about the camaraderie he enjoyed at Camp Seminole, as well as how much all that fun meant to him. He learned to shoot rifles there, and he clearly had very fond feelings for the place.

Another person with whom I spoke was Gresh Marsh, a retired educator himself. I talked on the phone with him about Camp Seminole on July 15, 2020, and during our talk, he revealed that his grandfather was Horace Marsh, the first football captain at Andrew Jackson High School—a most interesting fact.

Gresh went to Camp Seminole when he was about fourteen years old, a student at John Gorrie Junior High. Every summer day, he would be picked up by a school bus that whisked him away to Orange Park, where the camp was located on a big spring. "The whole camp was a lot of fun, but what I remember most was that the water was ice cold."

He recalled that the children were divided into four major groups named for Native American tribes: Cherokee, Choctaw, Shawnee and Chickasaw. These groups would compete in a variety of activities. There were rowboat races, swimming events and archery contests. The winning team was awarded the honor of having its flag displayed on a flagpole for the day—just enough incentive to encourage friendly competition among the campers.

Gresh also remembered that a lady came and made sandwiches for the children. Sometimes it was lettuce and tomato sandwiches, and other times it was meat sandwiches. He said that Tim Toomey got to have two meat sandwiches every day, an interesting but odd fact Gresh remembered.

Regardless of the menu, the days at Camp Seminole were filled with great fun and happiness. Those who got to go there, especially Gresh, were very lucky and happy to hold memories of such a time and place so close to home.

Ellen Shanks Rosenblum, a camper I mentioned earlier, remembers that in the late '50s, she attended the day camp called Camp Seminole. She would meet at her church, First Methodist, on Duval Street, to ride a school bus to the camp. Her most outstanding memory was of a spring that had a dock built all the way around it. She has since tried to locate the old campground, but there is a subdivision on the site now.

David Cameron is another happy camper from Camp Seminole. We spoke on the phone on August 1, 2020, and he told me about a very different aspect of Camp Seminole. In the summer between David's junior and senior year, 1961, he went every weekday with a group to Camp Seminole for a music camp. Clem Boatright was the choral director at what was then called Forrest High School and is now Westside High. Boatright took a group of singers with him in a yellow school bus, and David was among them. David loved the experience, and he recalled that after choral practice, they would all get to swim and enjoy tomato and mayonnaise sandwiches for lunch.

Camp Seminole may be one of those places that came and went and left little evidence of its existence, but too many people can tell stories about it. That shows that Camp Seminole had a real effect on many young people in the area back in the day. I know there are several folks who are glad that they got to experience such a happy place and time, and for that reason alone, I had to include Camp Seminole in this collection.

CAMP TOMAHAWK

*I*t was a gloomy day when I visited Alejandro Garces Camp Tomahawk Park, or the place we just called Camp Tomahawk when we were kids. It took me a while to find the location, since it is now surrounded by residences. Still, the place has several excellent hiking trails that are serene and beautiful. As I walked along, however, all I could hear was the traffic from nearby roads and NAS Jax aircraft flying over at regular intervals. As for wildlife, I did see some squirrels and a red-shouldered hawk. The most exciting thing I saw was a blue heron as he took off through the gray branches of the wintery woods. Otherwise, I was alone with my thoughts.

This was the place where many went to day camp, and Steve Baranak was one of those kids. Steve remembers that one summer, back when Camp Tomahawk was surrounded by undeveloped forest, he and his younger brother David got in a van that would pick them up every morning near the Resurrection School in Arlington. With about ten other campers, they would ride to the wilds of the San Jose area to a woodsy area called Camp Tomahawk.

Each day, he recalled, was devoted to one major activity. There was archery one day, arts and crafts another, canoeing and kayaking on still others and swimming—every day included swimming.

He reminisced that even though he was really young, he was a pretty good swimmer because he went with his family to Mike Roess Gold Head Branch State Park a lot. He got to swim at Camp Tomahawk, and he advanced quickly to the highest level of swimming proficiency. He also remembered a number of mock rescues in which he participated. Of course, anything

Camp Tomahawk campers on a hike, 1994. *Courtesy of the* Florida Times-Union.

that involved a swimming pool got Steve's attention. (When I went there, the park no longer had a pool.)

Canoeing was also pretty cool, he told me. There were expeditions down Goodby's Creek, although, getting in and out of the brackish water did cause him a bit of concern. He just didn't enjoy putting his feet into a body of water where he couldn't see the bottom or where he couldn't see where he was stepping.

Camp Tomahawk turned out to have left him with many pleasant sensations. It got him "far away" from his neighborhood. He also remembers looking at the older boys and wishing he could be as wise and mature as they appeared. He just couldn't wait to be fifteen, and Camp Tomahawk lives in his memory as a very wonderful time!

Another person with whom I talked was Victoria Ketchum. On July 14, 2020, we talked on the phone, and she related to me her camping memories. She was probably in the eighth grade in the late '60s when she went to a place she dearly loves—Camp Tomahawk.

"It was an awesome experience for me!" she told me with great enthusiasm. "I just loved it! There was so much to do and learn. There was archery and swimming, and even horseback riding, my very favorite. I learned to make baskets and learned to play chess and to tie knots. I loved it!"

Her family had just recently moved to Lakewood, and every summer day of that year, she got on a school bus and traveled the short distance to this wonderful place. She was able to expand her horizons as well as make many friends.

My friend Margo Dovi Feichmeir, who was mentioned earlier, had this to say about Camp Tomahawk in an email to me:

> *As for camps, Rick* [her brother] *& I went to a day camp when we were younger called Camp Tomahawk. I looked it up and it's a park now, but has an interesting Jacksonville history. The swimming "hole" must have been spring-fed, and I recall having to put alcohol drops in my ears after swimming each time. I was never the camp type. My youngest, Nora, is the only one of my kids who was enthusiastic about being dirty, sometimes cold, and sleeping with a bunch of snoring kids in the same room! I think she would have been a counselor if ballet hadn't taken over her life by high school.*

On Jacksonville's website, Camp Tomahawk was created and run by Octavio Garces and his wife, Geraldine, beginning in the late '50s. The camp was located off San Clerc Road between San Jose Boulevard and the

Camp Tomahawk counselor explaining the wild animals of the camp, 1994. *Courtesy of the Florida Times-Union.*

Beauclerc section of the city. It maintained its rustic natural state even when the camp closed and the City of Jacksonville bought the property in 1981 to use as a public park.

Garces was an instructor at the Bolles School, and the campers called him Captain O.S. Garces. When he sold the property to the city, he stipulated that the camp park be called Alejandro Garces Camp Tomahawk Park to honor his father.

The website went on to say that there was some push back over the sale of the property to the city. Some of the neighboring property owners were afraid that the park would attract vagrants. After much discussion and assurances, the park was left in a natural state with "a mature growth of oak, pine, and maple trees and a creek that extends through the middle of the tract to Goodbys Creek. And with help from the Mayor's Council on Fitness and Well-Being, the Jacksonville Track Club, and numerous Eagle Scouts, the trails have been expanded and improved over the years."

I am glad that this piece of property still stands undisturbed and that anyone can go for a hike there when the park is open, but this "camp" seems to be a shadow of its former self. Sadly, that is how the world goes—a constant dance of changes and our adjusting to them. And so it is with camps.

CAMPING CULTURE

Fireside Tales

*A*nother interesting facet of the camping experience has to be the stories that are often told. They are often related around the campfire, but sometimes they are told in the tent when the lights are out and there is little to protect the listening campers from "the evil that lurks" in the deep shadows of the woods. There is always the obligatory ghost story about the couple visiting Lovers' Lane when they are interrupted by a loud scratching on the door of the car, and when they quickly leave their spot and stop some miles away, they find the hook of a one-armed man dangling from the doorknob of the car, dripping with the blood of his latest victim. Oh, my!

But there is something about the wilderness that brings out the primal fear in a kid, and there is also a kind of joy that makes scaring one another to death a camping constant. In Nira Sue Trammel's book *Front Porch Tales*, she relates a great story about her sister and ghost stories and the campers at Camp Echockotee:

> *At the first opportunity in a new summer season, in the Stygian dark of night, we would play a mean trick on any newcomers to the camp. After a council ring session, we would lure them deep into the woods and then run off and leave them to make their way back to the compound.*
>
> *The favorite place for the desertion would be where McGirt the pirate was supposed to have been hanged. This was deep in the woods on the river bank near an old abandoned shack. Jane would have used her storytelling skills on the hike to the scene to scare them half out of their minds.*

There was always something very satisfying about watching those scouts come out of the woods, most of them crying and hysterical. We waited and hid in the bushes at the head of the white sand trail to count the bodies that passed in the night to be sure they all made it back okay.

Another scary story that was circulated around Camp Echockotee was about possible monkey escapes from the "Monkey Farm." On June 5, 1988, the *Florida Times-Union* published an article written by Bill Foley, a longtime and beloved columnist of the newspaper. It was titled, "Monkey Farm's Fame Fanned Out with Hairy Arms," and it proved that overactive imaginations of campers at Camp Echockotee were always ripe for stories about escaped apes raging through the undergrowth toward the boys as they gathered each summer.

According to Foley's article:

There was not much to Orange Park in those days. It was a sun-splashed village of bright flowers and dazzling waters. Staid home to the elderly at Moosehaven, raucous, character building playground for youth at Camp Echockotee. News files tell us the Yerkes Laboratories for Primates Research comprised 182 wooded acres on Kingsley Avenue about where the Foxwood subdivision is today. There was a 10 acre steel walled compound and what went on there was little known in the community, by the choosing of those secreted within. The locals called it Monkey Hill.

Foley went on to say that the Yerkes Laboratory was part of Emory University as well as being a "respected affiliate of Yale University and described as the second-oldest laboratory for primate research."

It seems that in 1930, Dr. Robert Mearns Yerkes, the author of the book *The Great Apes*, established his primate laboratory in Orange Park. Foley said that during World War I, Dr. Yerkes was involved with intelligence testing, and rumor was that it was here in his lab in OP that his scientists were able to perfect the frontal lobotomy procedure, taking "hysterical" primates and turning them into docile animals.

Actually, no one knew for sure what was going on in there, but that didn't stop the populace from being unnerved by the high steel walls, and it was small wonder that the place was always "shrouded in mystery compounded by myth." The high walls with electrified wire on top didn't do much to dissuade people, especially highly suggestible children, from being terrified of the place. All of this helped foster a mysterious reputation.

In any case, one of the first things boys heard on their first night at Camp Echockotee was that an ape had escaped from the "Monkey Farm," which is what the kids called it. Foley said:

> *Forget science. Forget Yale. Forget playful little monkeys. Forget intelligence test and frontal lobotomies. We are talking gorillas here. Great apes. Mad, hairy monsters thrashing through the underbrush smashing all before them, their only intent was to crush the spleens of fleeing children. Mad, unstoppable, invincible apes.*

Foley surmises that it was the mid-century B-movie mentality that made these stories so delightfully frightful, and the stories varied from campfire to campfire. Sometimes the story had one ape, sometimes more and always "just beyond the limits of perception, there was Something Out There, something from behind those walls."

Camp Echockotee was not, however, the only place where scary tales were told as children faced the prospect of another night in the deep, dark woods. According to Cindy Mathieson, it was at scouting trips at Camp Chowenwaw that she learned of the feared "Katty Wompus." This evil entity was reported to sneak into Scout tents at night without a soul knowing that it had been there. Of course, its stalking was just a prank played on "newbies," rather like an initiation. The sleeping and unsuspecting target would find big red whiskers drawn on her face with lipstick that had been smuggled in. Since there were no mirrors at camp—none in the Kiwashi and none in the tents, the victim would not realize that she had been marked until much later. Cindy also happened to mention to me that her mother was an Avon lady, and she had access to many small samples of the stuff in her mother's car. Very interesting.

At Camp Immokalee, where my daughter Amanda Ruland went on Indian Princess camping trips, she heard a story that stayed with her all these years. Seems there was a man driving on a lonely highway when he saw a beautiful but distressed young woman walking along the side of the road. He stopped and offered the girl a ride, and she accepted. She told him that her date left her for another girl at the dance and she was quite heartsick. The man took the girl home, and by that time she was composed and calm and very grateful to the man for his kindness. The next day, the man went by her house to check on her, only to have the mother of the girl become very confused since her daughter had died twenty years prior.

On July 7, 1994, the *Florida Times-Union* ran a story written by Ann Hyman titled "Tales of the Seaweed Witch and popping eyes." In it she tells of a creature that used to stalk Camp Weed, "the Episcopal Diocese of Florida's erstwhile getaway on the Gulf Coast near Tallahassee."

She said this creature would deposit in a camper's cot "wet, tangled seaweed, the odor of saltwater mud flats and dead fish clinging to its tendrils!" Apparently, everyone eventually got to know the "Seaweed Witch's" wrath. And when the camp moved to Lake City, she miraculously stopped her harassment of campers.

Not all scary stories deal with ghosts and witches. Sometimes more practical issues scare us. Patrick Hiney told me one that made me laugh:

> *The closest I can get to a scary event was running out of drinking water from home. The only water that was available at Camp Echockotee was sulfurated water, an elixir which, to this day, brings me closer to nausea than I care to come. I asked my parents to bring me some water from home on visiting day, but they didn't get my letter in time. Somehow I survived.*

The last scary memory is mine, and it dealt with my visits to Camp Montgomery as a kid. When I first went there, I couldn't have been much over thirteen. I would have undoubtedly gone with my church's youth group, the Pioneers, and as I recall, I had a wonderful time while there—no bad issues or problems. Boys were not yet on my radar, so I was mostly impressed with bonfires and games and sing-alongs and skits.

There was one little thing that was a bit disconcerting, however. Tucked between two cabins was a small, fenced-in piece of ground, ten feet by ten feet or so. In the center was a white stone grave marker that had a carved rose in bas relief at the top. The words on the stone read

EDDIE DAMMERS LOW.
DIED AT CRYSTAL LAKE FLA.
APR. 13. 1877.
AG. 6 YEARS. 8 MO.

I was understandably relieved when I realized that my cabin was at the far end of the camp and nowhere near this little grave, but as the years have gone by, I often think of little Eddie and how he came to be memorialized on the property of this camp. We were told that he had drowned in the lake long before there were any campers learning to swim or to canoe there. I could only imagine the sorrow that this little piece of property must have created in the Low family, so much so that it was a condition of the sale of

Grave marker of Eddie Dammers Low at Camp Montgomery, 2020. *Author's collection.*

the property to the Suwannee Presbytery (later to be named the Presbytery of St. Augustine) that the marker be kept where it was and that it be taken care of as long as the Presbytery owned the land.

I suppose that this is really a good place to spend the rest of eternity. Vibrant camp activities occur all year round at Camp Montgomery, with children and adults coming to church retreats and summer camp sessions.

The sounds of laughing and cheering and singing would be as good as the sounds of the heavenly hosts for a little boy whose life was cut short back in an April 1877.

Eddie never haunted me or any person I have asked who has been to Camp Montgomery, but his little grave certainly serves as a reminder that life is fleeting. Eddie Dammers Low has for the last 143 years silently urged the children who have haunted his Camp Montgomery to "seize the day" and "gather ye rosebuds while ye may," and all those similar quotations that encourage the living to make the most of their days. And if you listen to the breezes through the pines on the property, you might just hear a little voice saying that life is good and needs to be experienced to the fullest. In that regard, I think the children have been "haunted" by Eddie for a very long time.

CAMP WEED

On October 28, 2020, I made my way to Live Oak, Florida. I was to conduct an interview with the director of the current Camp Weed, but somehow communications got crossed and the director was in Jacksonville while I was in Live Oak. Gina Hoover of the office staff cheerfully filled in, and she supplied me with a great deal of information and many photographs. Afterward, she allowed me to wander the campus unescorted, and I was able to take pictures of anything I wanted. What had started as a difficult time ended up being quite a beautiful day.

One of the reports Gina gave me said that Camp Weed had at least six different locations in its lifetime. An unidentified camper wrote:

> *The first one* [camp] *ever was held at North Beach in St. Augustine for one week in the summer of 1923, the summer I was sixteen. I remember we drove the old brick road to St. Augustine and we took a passenger ferry across North Bay. We got into an open coach on rails pulled by a horse, and traveled across the swamp and the marshes and came out on a beautiful wild beach populated by mosquitoes.*
>
> *What I remember most about that first camp was that I had to keep interrupting my surf fishing to go to some kind of class or other.*

The other history provided me said that an Episcopal camp began in 1924—that the Diocese of Florida officially sponsored a camping experience

Left: Camp Weed at its Beacon Beach location (around 1938). *Courtesy of Camp Weed and Cerveny Conference Center.*

Right: Bishop Edwin Gardener Weed, the Third Bishop of the Episcopal Diocese of Florida, 1920s. *Courtesy of Camp Weed and Cerveny Conference Center.*

for forty boys and girls at a beach near St. Augustine. These kids were from the Young People's Service Leagues in Jacksonville. Either way, a camping experience was going to be provided for young people of the diocese.

In 1925, the second camp formed when it moved to St. Andrews Bay near Panama City, on the west coast of Florida. It was at this location that the camp received the name Camp Weed. The camp was named for Edwin Garner Weed, the third bishop of Florida. At this new location, the daily schedule included early morning worship services, classes until lunchtime and afternoons filled with recreation followed by evenings around a campfire.

Four years later, the third camp formed in 1929. The diocese purchased ten acres overlooking the bay at Beacon Beach of Florida. It was fortunate that the property had a former hotel and four screened bungalow cottages, which they were able to convert for camping. By 1930, 130 youngsters as well as Sunday school teachers and church leaders began enjoying sessions offered at this Camp Weed.

By 1940, there were over four hundred people in attendance in camp sessions, so the experience was proving very enjoyable, but World War II was about to break out. The U.S. Army found it necessary to take control of the Beacon Beach property. St. Joe Paper Company presented the diocese with beautiful property on St. James Bay at St. Teresa Beach, but it also was taken by the U.S. Army. During the four years that followed, the fourth Camp Weed operated at Hibernia on the St. John's River, a place in Clay County near Green Cove Springs.

When the war was over, the property was relinquished to the diocese, and the camp's fifth location was back at the Gulf Coast to St. Teresa Beach in

Iconic cross at Camp Weed, St. Theresa Beach location, 1967. *Courtesy of the Florida State Photographic Archives.*

1946. As a form of compensation for using the land, one could assume, the army left barracks, mess halls and offices, all of which were quickly converted to the campers' use. The camp thrived through the rest of the '40s, '50s, and '60s with constant growth and scope of programs, but this was taking a toll on the facilities.

By 1970, there was a need to find a more centrally located camp, since this property was right on the border of another diocese. A search was authorized in 1976, and the St. Teresa location was sold. A five-hundred-acre property on White Lake near Live Oak was purchased and would become the sixth camp. Tents were used for several summer sessions, but in 1981, the first permanent facilities were erected, and in 1983, the camp could boast a kitchen, a dining room and cabins. In 1995, Mandi's Chapel was begun as a memorial to the life of Amanda Petway, daughter of Thomas Petway III and Elisabeth Herdman Petway of Jacksonville, Florida.

I was not able to locate an obituary for Amanda, but I found a tribute written by her friend Molly Brandhorst McMahon. It was published on The College Today: The Official News Site of the College of Charleston, and it was most touching. It read in part:

> *Mandi Petway had a sparkle. She just did. She treasured each day and each friend with a certainty, which was inspiring. Together, we experienced many firsts at the College, and we enjoyed being constantly surrounded by laughter. A positive attitude—just one of Mandi's many incredible qualities—would prove to be her secret weapon against an illness she would battle for her four years at the College. Mandi's deep faith was also mature for a college student and was a tremendously encouraging example to me at a time of my life when I was most impressionable.*
>
> *Mandi graduated from the College in 1990. Her battle with cancer ended just a few years later, when she was called to heaven to dance with the angels.*

The chapel that was built in Mandi's honor is spectacular and seems almost too fancy for a camp, but it certainly captures the "sparkle quality" that Amanda must have possessed. The chapel's architect was John Zona, and the structure, built out over the lake, was built in 1995. It is so striking that it won Top Religious Building in 2012 and Second Overall Building in 2012 in a competition sponsored by the Florida Chapter of the American Institute of Architects.

Above: Diving and swimming fun at Camp Weed, at its St. Theresa location, 1967. *Courtesy of the Florida State Photographic Archives.*

Left: Mandy's Chapel at Camp Weed, 2020. *Author's collection.*

Camp Weed's current entrance in Live Oak, Florida, 2020. *Author's collection*.

Today, the Live Oak location of Camp Weed (now called Camp Weed and Cerveny Conference Center) is spectacular. Entering the grounds, I was struck immediately by the beauty of the towering oak canopy, dripping with Spanish moss. The light filtered through the branches very nicely, and I passed by numerous well-tended meadows and fields that would be ideal for any number of sports or games.

All along the road to the office, there were some unusual structures that at first glance I thought were places to display information. Soon, I realized that they were old stained-glass church windows. Gina Hoover took the time to research their journey for me. She found that Benjamin Hill was instrumental in saving the windows taken from a disbanded Episcopal church—St. Mark's Episcopal Church in Chattahoochee, Florida. The design of the panes of glass was very simple, colorful and illuminated at night. I could imagine these serving as beautiful beacons along the campers' way.

The architecture of the Office, Registration and Conference Center seemed new and very well-maintained. When I arrived, a crew was landscaping the grounds near the office, and there were workers pressure-washing the decks between buildings. This place is more than just a summer

One of several stained-glass windows placed along the roadway at Camp Weed. These windows were saved from demolition by Benjamin Hill when St. Mark's Episcopal Church in Chattahoochee, Florida, was closed, 2020. *Author's collection*.

camp. It is used for many functions throughout the Episcopal Diocese of Florida, and it appears to be a very busy place. The Cerveny Conference Center was named for the Bishop Frank Cerveny, the sixth bishop of the state of Florida.

On June 9, 2020, I spoke on the phone with Angela Corey about her time at Camp Weed. Some of her happiest memories took place the Camp Weed, located at St. Theresa Beach on the Gulf of Mexico. This camp was situated in such a way that campers could see Alligator Point from the banks of the camp, and in some places, it had pine tree forests that grew all the way down to the water's edge.

For one summer in senior high, she was a camper, but during her last summer there, she was a counselor. As Angela described it, Camp Weed "was stunningly beautiful with its iconic cross towering in God's beautiful space." So many happy things happened to her while there that she couldn't even pinpoint any specific event.

She mostly remembers all the wonderful activities of which she was a part. There were dances at the huge Recreational Hall, and there were sports of all kinds to play. She remembers teaching some of the campers how to sail in little Sunfish sailboats, long before the fear of sharks existed. She mentioned the "buddy checks" the lifeguards would call when everyone was in the water. One had better hold up his partner's hand, or heads would roll.

One activity she recalled was when campers would canoe down one of the local rivers and then land their boats where they would set up their tents right on the beach. Then, they would prepare their meat, potato and vegetable dinners in tinfoil packets that they placed on their fire. Delicious!

Another time that she remembered fondly was when she was the coach of a little boys' baseball team, and they won the tournament. "It was one big mound of happiness!"

Sadly, when Angela was heading down to Tampa recently, she discovered that her Camp Weed had been converted to condominiums, and the amazing place where she had camped and coached, worshiped and counseled was a camp no more. Angela wasn't sure if the entire property had been developed, and she plans on a future expedition to see if any part of her youthful experience still lingers. Still, the impact of Camp Weed summers cannot be eradicated, and this place of wonder and joy still exists in the hearts of many campers, regardless of the location. Angela would just love the Camp Weed of today.

"Camp Weed was an amazing and positive place for me," she said, and from the sound of her voice, I was could tell that it certainly was, for her and countless others throughout northeast Florida.

CAMP WIL-LE-MA AND OTHERS

I wanted to point out another sad fact of life—most of us are very careless with our histories as we live them. It would have been so great if we had kept those handbooks and manuals. If only we had thought to store all those badges and camp-made trinkets. Why didn't we take more pictures and then keep them safely in shoeboxes? If only we had not lost them in a move to college or a first house.

Even more distressing is that many organizations are not much better about saving old things than individuals are. They are often too busy getting things accomplished, so they forget to carefully save old rosters or pamphlets or pictures so that the history of a place can be preserved. Too often when I call a camp office, the young staff member has no idea what happened earlier than one summer before, and the older staff member often has forgotten where old documents can be found. And sometimes what is saved is not dated or preserved in any formal way. In my experience, people often pull out boxes of ephemera from closets that haven't been touched in years.

This reality came home to me when I spoke with Kathy Colvin, a teacher friend of mine. We spoke in a telephone interview on June 18, 2020, and she told me she was a Camp Fire Girl who had spent a summer or two in Live Oak, Florida, at a Camp Fire Girl camp. Kathy had a sensation, when thinking of camp, that many campers I have interviewed have had. It is the sensation that camping was wonderful and liberating, but there were no specific events or incidents to which they could point to prove that fact.

"It is interesting that I felt like it was a very BIG experience," she told me. "I feel like I found my bliss there." Beyond that, she could only recall small details.

When Kathy was about ten and a Blue Bird in the organization, her mother would take her to W.T. Grants Department Store, where she would buy enough assorted materials to make six little girl shirts and six little girl shorts. These Kathy could get as dirty as she pleased because they were not meant to last past the end of camp. She also got a new pair of Keds, and she was all set.

She got on a big yellow school bus and headed to far away Live Oak, where her camp was located. Her brother was probably going to Camp Echockotee with the Boy Scouts, she told me.

The camp, as Kathy recalled, was rustic, with very old buildings, and she thought that the camp might have been on the banks of the Suwannee River. She wasn't certain. She did recall that there were bunk beds, and they cooked their breakfast on little stoves that they made out of paraffin and tin cans. Toast was prepared on a stick over the fire. She remembers painting things and making things out of wood, but she wasn't sure what she was making or why she was making it. It was just fun to do. She also remembered the word *WOHELO*, which stood for Work, Health, Love, but she wasn't sure how it figured into her experience.

She also marveled at the fact that she had no sunscreen and no bug spray. How she managed stay alive was anybody's guess. Still, in a week's time, she was back home. Although there may not be a monumental moment to this camping experience, Kathy had no horror stories or broken bones. She even went on to become a camp counselor at another camp when she was sixteen. Still, she was able to "find her bliss," and that has to count for something!

I went on to research what I could about this campsite by going to the website for the Camp Fire organization. It said that Camp Fire Girls was founded by Dr. Luther Halsey Gulick and his wife, Charlotte Vetter Gulick, in 1910, two years before the Girls Scouts were formed. As a matter of fact, when I went to Wikipedia concerning the history of Camp Fire Girls, I found that it was in 1907 when the Gulicks had established Camp WoHeLo, on Lake Sebago, near South Casco, Maine. By 1910, seventeen girls went there for camping. The Wiki article went on to say that the Girl Scouts and Camp Fire Girls were to merge into Camp Fire Pioneers, but there was a division and the two groups went their separate ways.

In any case, the Camp Fire Girls organization wanted to provide girls with outdoor learning experiences to help "guide young people on their journey to self discovery." The Camp Fire website said that it was the first multiracial, multicultural and nonsectarian organization for girls. In 1975, it became co-educational, and sexual orientation was added to its inclusion policy in 1998. Today, there are fifty-four chapters or "councils" of Camp Fire participants.

With all of this in mind, I continued to search for Kathy's Camp Fire Girls' Camp but had a great deal of difficulty finding where it might have been. Even the national organization of Camp Fire in Kansas City said that a Live Oak camp no longer exists. Today, there are only two major Camp Fire Councils in North Florida—one in Lakeland and the other in Pensacola. The camp in Live Oak, I was told, might have been leased by the organization in earlier times, but there was no written record they could find for me concerning a Live Oak location.

There was one lucky accident for me when I just happened upon several news articles about a Camp Fire camp in Jacksonville. The first article I found was published in the *Jacksonville Journal* on March 17, 1972, and there is mention of a camp in the Fort Caroline area called Camp Wil-Le-Ma (spelled and capitalized variously by contemporary sources). They were going to have a celebration of Camp Fire's sixty-seventh birthday. I was unable to tell when this Fort Caroline camp formed, however.

Then, I found another article about the Jacksonville site. In the *Florida Times-Union* on April 25, 1983, an article ran titled "Camp Fire Plans Eight Camping Sessions." It said:

> *North Florida Council of Camp Fire Inc. will open its resident camp Wil-le-ma, 13165 Mount Pleasant Road, on June 19, for eight 1-week camping sessions, continuing through Aug. 13.*
>
> *Sessions are open to boys and girls ages 6-14. Activities will include swimming, arts, crafts, sports, nature hikes, outdoor cooking, camp lore, songfests, "dancercize" and outdoor living.*

In another article I found published in the *Jacksonville Journal* on April 3, 1984, about a year later, it showed that things were not going well with the Camp Fire organization in Jacksonville. The United Way had cut off funding to the North Florida Camp Fire Council, and that meant that about 75 percent of the local organization's revenue had dried up. One of the reasons United Way removed its funding was mentioned in the article. It said that:

The council had been fighting declining membership for more than 15 years. At one time it had over 2000 members. But in 1968 its membership had dropped to 800. Now [1984] the council has 191 girls and boys.

At this time, the United Way was contributing $500 per member, and when they compared that amount to what other Camp Fire groups in the nation were getting, they found that there was a vast discrepancy. The average amount contributed to other camps was only $74 per camper. This is apparently why the money was withdrawn by the United Way.

Undeterred, local Camp Fire officials vowed to raise enough money to continue on their own, but clearly, there was no way to generate the kind of money they needed with dues and garage sales. The sale of the camp property was probably the only way to generate enough money to pay debts or to carry on. News of the sale of Camp Wil-Le-Ma finally came in the *Florida Times-Union* on July 6, 1984. According to the article written by Jesse-Lynne Kerr:

> *The North Florida Council of Camp Fire Inc. sold its camp on Mount Pleasant Road in an effort to recoup funds lost when the United Way discontinued sponsorship of the agency earlier this year.*
>
> *The Nature Conservancy bought the 16.72 acre Camp Wil-le-ma [sic] which adjoins the 603-acre Theodore Roosevelt Preserve.*
>
> *Neither buyer nor seller would disclose the purchase price, but documentary stamps attached to the deed in county records show a sale price of $200,000.*

These articles made clear to me that these wonderful organizations took a great deal of money to run and to maintain. We children were oblivious to the monetary demands required to make our summer lives so full, and I for one am grateful I lived in a time when such experiences were within the grasp of most kids.

Camp Wil-Le-Ma was not Kathy's camp, but it seems likely that her camp in Live Oak suffered a similar fate to the one in Jacksonville. Because the national Camp Fire organization cannot locate any information about the Lake City camp, we will never know for certain. In any case, Kathy found her bliss somewhere in a northeast Florida camp, and for that we can all be glad.

MUSIC, DRAMA, ART
AND MORE

*N*ot all children of earlier generations wanted to spend their time outdoors. There were those who preferred less hot, less buggy and less strenuous indoor activities. They did not, however, want to spend their entire summers at Grandma's or at home getting in their parents' hair. These kids wanted to have the non-school bonding experience that alternative camps had to offer, and Jacksonville kids had a variety of these experiences from which to choose. Art camps, music camps and drama camps are a few of the indoor camps that people I interviewed shared with me. Most of these people had a desire to develop talents they already had, or they wanted to experience activities in a less academic setting as they enjoyed their vacation.

On May 30, 2020, Claire Fleming King and I spoke on the phone about her band camp experience. Claire was able to attend the Gatorland Music Clinic, July 1966, at University of Florida. In 1966, Claire was a senior when she went to the summer band camp at University of Florida run by Richard Bowles, the band director of university and a real celebrity in the world of marching bands at the time. The one hundred or so summer camp band members stayed in the dorms on campus since most college students would be home for the summer. Her roommate was Myra Houston, who also was from Wolfson High School.

This camp was the first time Claire had ever played in an integrated band. Claire remembered that her hardest competition was from a girl from William M. Raines High School by the name of Rene Lilly. Both girls

Band Camp at University of Florida, 1966. *Courtesy of Claire Fleming King.*

wanted to be first chair for the flute, and they were extremely competitive about it. Eventually, they became friends.

Band members had little time on their own. The band camp program filled their evenings with concerts, plays and musicals like *The Fantastics*, a most memorable experience for Claire. During the times not practicing on the field, the program directors filled the hours with private lessons and practice sessions in the music rooms provided. Claire also mentioned how tough the thirty or so chaperones and teachers were. There wasn't much time for shenanigans.

Claire said, "I came away from the camp so much better as a musician and person." It may have lasted only two weeks and was quite expensive— many hours of babysitting money were needed to supplement her parents'

contribution—but she loved the opportunity to be on her own. At the end, her parents came down for the final performance, and then they went back to Jacksonville together. "It was a very wonderful thing."

There was another type of innovative summer camp for those kids who preferred indoor activities. The Little Theatre of Jacksonville, now called Theatre Jacksonville, offered a great summer activity for several summers running—Drama Camp. Participants were able to learn all manner of stagecraft and then perform a show for family and friends as a culminating activity.

My daughter Amanda Ruland was between the sixth and seventh grades in 1987 when she was involved with a drama camp. She recalls that she played the wicked stepmother in *Cinderella with a Twist*, a 1950s retelling of the classic fairy tale of Cinderella.

Drama Camp at Theatre Jacksonville, 1986. *Author's collection*.

"Oh, my gosh, I really loved that summer!" she told me in a phone interview on September 23, 2020. She loved that every morning the group of which she was a part would go onto the stage of the theater or out to the little park in the center of San Marco in order to practice lines and block out their scenes.

"One of the most fun exercises I can remember was supervised by Robert Arleigh White. He would have us repeat unintelligible phrases with certain types of inflection so that we would see that our tones of voice can communicate a tremendous amount of information. We would say something unrecognizable with an angry voice or a scared voice or a sexy voice. We did a lot of laughing as I recall. And Mr. White really helped me understand about how body language communicates more than you think. He was the best teacher ever!"

Amanda also loved that she got to dress up in all the costumes that they stored in the back of the Little Theatre. In preparing for her play, she had lots of poodle skirts and crinolines from which to choose, and the makeup was "amazing." She explained that it had to be very "overdone" so that people in the audience could make out the actor's features.

"Boy, I really miss those days!" she told me at the end of our conversation.

Another drama camp participant was Lindsay Turner. We also talked by telephone on September 23, 2020, about her "run" at Theatre Jacksonville's Drama Camp when she was about eight or nine in the mid-'90s.

"It's funny," she told me. "When I was little and I was at home, I could sing and dance like Shirley Temple, but when I walked into the drama camp and saw all these kids that I did not already know, I became like a turtle. I really was just too shy to show my true colors."

Thankfully for her, she warmed up and she really began to enjoy the experience. Eventually, she was a member of the crowd in the production of *FAME*. Even now she could sing a few bars of "I'm going to live forever." And thankfully, her fond memories of summer camp will "live forever" as well.

Another kind of camp to which children had access was the one held at the old Children's Museum. Pamela Lea and I talked on the telephone on May 26, 2020, about a summer camp I had no idea even existed. It was held in the old Children's Museum on Riverside Avenue. It lasted all day: and participants were able to engage in a variety of arts, crafts and behind-the-scenes activities in the museum and around Riverside.

As Pamela recalled, there was a carriage house out in the back of the building that held some animals that they were able to pet and to feed. They could wander about the planetarium and the scary attic, which held many things that were not currently on display.

Pamela said, "I remember them taking us all out on Riverside Avenue and all of us kids all lined up and sitting on the sidewalk with our art pads. We were to draw what we saw to the right of us with our right hands. Then were to draw what we saw to the left of us with our left hand."

There were scientific things the kids got to try. Lea mentioned the "ever-popular baking soda rocket" as an example. But she really loved anything to do with rocks. She recalled that someone came and helped them break open geodes, and that was miraculous when they got to see what was inside. She was so taken with rocks she bought a box of them at the gift shop. It had about ten rocks inside, and she was thrilled.

When Pamela was older, she went to the Art Camp at the Art Museum on Art Museum Drive. Not only did they get to be "nose-to-nose" with bona fide pieces of art, but she and her companions also learned how to make things with papier mâché. They got to experiment with ceramics and try their hands at painting. When the end of the camp came, each student's art was listed for sale in a catalogue, just like a real artist. There was even a show with refreshments.

They also got to meet artists like Lee Adams, a famous Jacksonville artist, whose work was very popular locally. They also got to meet world-famous Peter Maxx, the psychedelic icon of the '60s, who had come to the Art

Museum for a fundraiser. He was there to sell his lithographs, one of which Pamela bought and has had for many years.

On May 1, 1975, the *Florida Times-Union* provided its readers with a list of summer day camps. I was shocked at how many opportunities children had to be enriched during their summers away from school. There were fourteen camps provided by the Jacksonville Recreational Department, and twenty-three camps were run by the Duval County School System. UNF had the Eastern and National Cheerleading camps; the Humane Society, the Jacksonville Zoo and some horseback-riding camps had opportunities for kids to work with animals. Jacksonville University ran a science camp, a dance camp and a fine arts camp. There were sports camps all over the area—tennis, baseball, soccer and basketball. The YMCA had camps going in Arlington, Beaches, Jessie Ball DuPont and Johnson Branch. There were computer camps and camps for children with special needs. Even Skate World ran a camp for skaters and the Rudder Club had a camp for sailing.

There was something for everybody in this "brave new world" of summer camping, and you would think that this would be a good thing. But it seems this marked the beginning of the decline of the one-week overnight summer camp phenomenon. These day camps were fun, inexpensive and often air-conditioned. The rough and rugged summer camps of old were not nearly as appealing when these close-to-home camps were temptingly available.

BITS AND PIECES
AND BABY JELLIES

*A*s often happens when one writes a book on a rather broad topic, there are some bits that do not quite fit in with the flow of the information, but these pieces of information are too interesting to leave out. That is why I included them in this chapter. These memories are priceless, as they say, and I would hate for any gems to be lost to posterity.

Margaret Rose, a longtime friend, contacted me in an email on June 6, 2020, when I was well into the manuscript of this book. She wanted to add her remembrances of summer camps. Hers was a day camp that was run by the Jacksonville Jewish Center when it was located at Third and Silver Streets. She wrote:

> I wanted to let you know I went to summer camp as a child at the Jacksonville Jewish Center, probably in the late 1950s, early 1960s when the synagogue was still located in Springfield on 3rd and Silver Street. The camp probably moved to Mandarin in the late 1960s when I became a counselor. I do remember the camp was on the property before the new synagogue was built.
>
> When camp was held at the old synagogue and there was no pool, I remember over the years we had swimming lessons in the basement of a church, I'm thinking maybe Good Shepherd, a motel on Phillips Highway, and a place we referred to as the "mudhole." I'm thinking it was a man-made lake. The director of the camp was Blanche Slott, who was the synagogue Executive Director at that time. She lived to be 102 years old and passed away in 2016.

I felt it was important to include Margaret's insights about camping, because they provided a glimpse into the everyday fabric of Jacksonville landmarks, people and activities.

The second story just made me laugh out loud. It also came to me in an email. On May 8, 2020, Charlotte Wynn's recollection arrived, and it was just too cute to leave out. She said:

I only attended one camp as a child, and it was in Leesburg (Lake Yale Baptist Camp). I lived in a rural area on the Northside of Jacksonville when I was 11 years old. This area of Jacksonville was a dairy community and was home to many dairies that serviced our city and surrounding areas. My father was the preacher at Dinsmore Baptist Church. We were poor although I was completely unaware of this fact because everyone I knew happened to be poor too. The church had raised money for 35 kids to attend a week-long visit to Lake Yale. We were all excited because most of us had never been away from our parents for a week or in most cases, ever been away anywhere.

My first morning at Camp began in the cafeteria and that's when I realized that I had never been to a restaurant or cafeteria for BREAKFAST in my life. As I slid my tray down the line making my selections, I noticed something I had never seen before. There, in a large bowl, were small (tiny even) individual packets of fruit jelly. Strawberry, grape, and blackberry! They were so cute and little. I thought of them as "Baby Jellies." I had never seen such! I was amazed that people could have such adorably packaged condiments for breakfast. I swiped a few and put them in my pocket. I couldn't wait to get back home to show my Mom what I'd discovered. For whatever reason, I thought she'd be as impressed and amazed as me.

I really couldn't wait until the end of the week when I would be returning home to show her my treasure. I decided to include them in my letter home to her that I'd be writing that day. In the letter, I begged her to remember to save them for me and not to let anyone else in the family eat them. At 11 years old I did not know that the US Postal Service used machines to sort (and in my case) stamp and flatten letters. At the end of the week, when I returned from Camp, I busted through the backdoor of my house with only one thing on my mind. The Baby Jellies. My Mama was there waiting and the first thing I asked was, "Did you get my letter?"

She went into the kitchen and pulled something down from the top of the refrigerator. It was in a piece of tin foil. She put it on the table and I unwrapped the stickiest mess of an envelope that you could ever imagine. The letter I had written was unreadable and the Baby Jellies were crushed and mangled. The address on the outside of the envelope was barely legible and I can't believe it was even able to be delivered.

My Mama said she figured it was from me but for the life of her didn't know what to do with it so she'd just saved it 'til I got home. If I had known the definition of the word, "crestfallen," I would have used it at that moment. My Mama felt bad for me and didn't even give me "The Look" when I complained for at least the next few weeks about our BIG grape jelly jar and how much I hated it. Going to camp gave me not only a peek of what life was like beyond my little world, but a true love of discovering the wonder of Baby Jellies and the joy they could bring.

There was no way I could leave these out. Imagining the Jewish campers swimming in the Good Shepherd swimming pool warmed my heart, and the lesson of the Baby Jellies is one that shall live in infamy, I suppose.

CAMPING CULTURE

Songs

America the Beautiful

O beautiful for spacious skies,
for amber waves of grain,
For purple mountains majesties
Above the fruited plain!
America! America!
God shed His light on thee,
and crown thy good with brotherhood
From sea to shining sea!

—*Katherine Lee Bates and Samuel A. Ward, in* Campfire Songs: Lyrics
and Chords to More Than 100 Sing-Along Favorites, *edited by Irene*
Maddox and Rosalyn Cobb

I don't recall when or how it was I learned campfire songs. It seems
to me that most of the songs sung around a fire were ones we already
knew, having learned them in school. We had to know the songs, since
carrying sheets of music out in the woods would have been impractical, even
difficult.

As I recall, back in the '50s and '60s, and probably even further back
than that, public school children sang at the beginning of each school
day. The one song I remember best was one we sang quite often, if not
every day—"America the Beautiful." It was all part of a "patriotic"

and "inspirational" time that also included a Bible verse or two and the recitation of "The Lord's Prayer."

Now, every time I hear "America the Beautiful," I feel a flush of patriotism and a pang of bitter sweetness. To be honest, though, my feelings may be as much about nostalgia as love for God and country. Who isn't moved by the lyrical beauty portrayed in this song—amber waves of grain, purple mountains and shining seas? Who doesn't flash back to the scrubbed, sweet faces of elementary friends as we raised our voices in schools that insisted we sing, every day?

I guess that is why I wanted to include a chapter on campfire songs in this book about northeast Florida summer camps. Songs were an integral part of the camping experience. Some songs were meant to provide a cadence to which campers could march or work. Other songs were sung in unison as campers encircled a fire after a day of intense activity. It was easy to enjoy joining with others in happy sounds. As C. Richard Leonard mentioned in an earlier chapter, he loved the camaraderie that campfire songs created when he was a Boy Scout at Camp Echockotee. Whether the songs were silly or deeply moving, singing them simply punctuated the end of a fun day of camping.

When I was at the Camp Chowenwaw Museum doing research, I found a book on one of the shelves in a display case. Its title was *Sing Together: A Girl Scout Songbook*, and it was published by the Girl Scouts of the U.S.A. in 1949. An inscription in the front said that the book had been purchased at a yard sale in Fleming Island, Florida, on June 12, 2020. Eventually, the book made its way to the Camp Chowenwaw Museum, and on that lovely day in August, I held it in my hand.

As I looked through the table of contents, I recognized many songs from my youth. Along with "America the Beautiful," there was "Home on the Range," "The Battle Hymn of the Republic," "Old King Cole," "Billy Boy" and "Blow the Man Down."

The book listed four different "Good Night," songs, along with "Au Clair de la Lune," and "Taps." There were five listings for songs to be sung before meals instead of saying grace. There were ten Girl Scout songs, none of which I recognized.

But there were many songs missing, I thought. I very distinctly remember singing "Waltzing Matilda" and "Kookaburra" when I went on camping trips. There were no listings for "Kumbayah," "Michael Row the Boat Ashore" or "There Were Ten in the Bed," all perennial favorites at Girl Scout Camp. I needed a different, more up-to-date book of songs, so I later purchased a book called *Campfire Songs: Lyrics and Chords to More Than 100 Sing-Along Favorites*. It was compiled by Irene Maddox and Rosalyn Cobb, and it was published in 1983.

In the introduction of their book, Maddox and Cobb said:

> *Many songs have been passed down from one generation to another. Melodies have been altered to fit the singer or the place, but the spirit of the music lives on, giving us songs to cheer us when we are down, inspire us when we are tired, and soothe us when we are troubled.*
>
> *Breaking into song wherever we are—in the car, in the shower, at work, or at play—is second nature to us. The songs we sing are usually the ones we remember from our parents or from our childhood songfests around a campfire.*

This book was filled with many familiar songs—"The Wheels on the Bus," "I Know an Old Lady Who Swallowed a Fly," "You Are My Sunshine," "Molly Malone" and "Swing Low Sweet Chariot"—These were just a sampling of the many other songs that bubbled up in my memory. And as I imagined each melody, I could very easily see all kinds of campers—Girl Scout campers, church youth group campers, Boy Scout campers or family campers—all singing and enjoying the wonders of a campfire at the closing of a day.

There are, however, two songs that were sung toward the end of all campfires. One is a song that I remember very tenderly from my camping days. It is one that my mother taught to my Girl Scout troop. Where it came from, I can't say for sure. In doing deeper research, I found on the internet a variety of places where these lyrics were posted. Nowhere was there any attribution for the author. At www.familii.com, I found this set of lyrics, and it was described as follows: "A folk song traditionally sung at scouting camps, this song was popular in both Canada and the United States during the 1950s and 60s."

Of course, when we Girl Scouts sang this song, we were absolutely bone tired. I suppose you would say that we didn't sing so much as mumbled the words by that time of night. We were then quick to hurry to our tents or cabins, where we collapsed into bedrolls and onto cots where we slept until the sun rose and reminded us that we were famished.

The song's words are:

> *Bed is too small for my tiredness.*
> *Give me a hilltop with trees.*
> *Tuck a cloud up under my chin.*
> *Lord, blow the moon out, please.*

There are other verses, but they are quite repetitive. Nothing beats the power of the first verse, however, and my guess is that this closing song was written by a tired mother somewhere at some distant time as she tried to coax her little ones to sleep. In any case, the song touches me deeply. I suppose that is because I associate it with my mother, and I like to think that she has found the peace for which the song seems to long. I know that thinking about the song and my mother and campfires does that for me.

The second song can actually bring tears to my eyes for a variety of reasons. It's sometimes called "Butterfield's Lullaby," but we know it better as "Taps."

According to an article written by Elizabeth Nix published on August 22, 2018, for www.history.com, "Taps" was written during the Civil War. "Taps" was the term soldiers used long ago for the three drumbeats sounded to signal "Lights Out" at the end of the day. General Daniel Butterfield of the Union army wanted something different, so he had his brigade bugler Private Oliver Wilcox Norton come up with a new bugle call that would serve the same purpose—to signal the troops to put the lights out and get some rest.

Norton came up with a twenty-four-note melody that Butterfield changed slightly before Norton played it for the first time for the men. Its plaintive sound must have touched many souls as it was carried on the winds of that night. It proved so popular that it wasn't long before other Union units were using it to signal the end of day. After a while, even the Confederate army could be heard playing the same song far away in their camps.

In 1862, after a seven-day battle at Harrison's Landing, Virginia, near Richmond, Virginia, "Taps" was played for the first time at a funeral that honored a fallen Union cannoneer. His commander was Captain John Tidwell, and Tidwell wanted something to be done to honor the dead man besides the three-rifle volley, which might sound like the beginning of another attack. "Taps" was played instead, and it proved so perfectly meaningful that it soon became part of military funerals.

Nira Sue Trammell had a most beautiful passage in her book *Front Porch Stories: Memories of Old Florida* that talked of her experiences with the music provided by a camp bugler. As you may remember, she was just a young girl living at Camp Echockotee, where her father served as a carpenter/builder for the camp. Trammell remembered:

> *A scout bugler would play Reveille around 6A.M. and then at sundown, Taps.*
> *I would sit, hidden from all eyes, beneath the stairs to the small platform*
> *on which the bugler stood for this morning and evening ritual. I never had to*

wait long since I was so familiar with the routine, but I always made sure I was out of sight by the time he arrived.

The moment was too private to allow anyone to share it with me. This is really the perfect way to begin and end a day and I will never forget the exquisite sensation, almost akin to sweetness, of hearing that bugler perform. My throat would convulse from emotion and tears would spring to my eyes because it was so beautiful.

My own experience with "Reveille" was not a happy one. My father, who had been a bugler in the Boy Scouts and in the U.S. Navy, once blasted the tune at me as I lay sleeping, and I almost had a heart attack.

"Taps," on the other hand, has always stirred me deeply when I hear it anywhere. We, however, did not have a bugler on any of our camping trips or summer camp sessions, so we had to wake ourselves up in the morning, and in the evening we had to sing "Taps."

Since it is never wise to trust one's memory, I consulted the internet to find the lyrics to "Taps." According to www.americansongwriter.com, these lyrics are sometimes attributed to Horace Lorenzo Trim, but there has been debate about whether that is absolutely accurate. After that, no one knows for certain who actually wrote the lyrics. The words on the website said that the title for the song is "Never Forget," and the words are as follows:

Never forget.

Day is done, gone the sun,
From the lake, from the hills, from the sky;
All is well, safely rest, God is nigh.

Fading light, dims the sight,
And a star gems the sky, gleaming bright.
From afar, drawing nigh, falls the night.

Thanks and praise, for our days,
'Neath the sun, 'neath the stars, neath the sky;
As we go, this we know, God is nigh.

Sun has set, shadows come,
Time has fled, Scouts must go to their beds
Always true to the promise that they made.

While the light fades from sight,
And the stars gleaming rays softly send,
To thy hands we our souls, Lord, commend.

Although, "America the Beautiful" is one camping song that churns up a great deal of emotion in me, it is "Taps" that really makes my eyes glisten. I respond to hearing it much like Nira Sue Trammell did when she would hear it played by a Boy Scout of a very distant time. I am so grateful that songs were part of my camping experiences. There can be little doubt that music sung by young voices enriched the camping experience for me and for many others.

CONCLUSION

*I*n the *Florida Times-Union* on July 13, 1972, an article ran titled "Summer Camps Periled." It touched on issues that had begun to plague the summer camp industry quite some time ago. According to the UPI article:

> *The summer camp business for boys and girls isn't near what it was five years ago; in fact for the most part it's terrible and hundreds of camps have closed.*
>
> *The American Camping Association says its membership of 3,300 summer camps in 1968 has dwindled by 600....*
>
> *Taxes and inflation have closed many. Taxes are up by 100 to 150 percent from the early 1960s, and the cost of food and counselor salaries has gone up at least as much.*

Add these facts to the changes in the climate of our culture—from one that requires much responsibility from its children to one that often pampers them to excess. Even Bill Foley saw the handwriting on the wall, so to speak. On May 1, 1995, in the *Florida Times-Union*, he said:

> *You can imagine my shock when I heard summer camp was being air-conditioned as well. Camp Immokalee in this case.*
>
> *YMCA camp near Keystone Heights. Cherished part of local heritage. Leaders of men molded there....*
>
> *Air-conditioned summer camp is preposterous. Absurd. Will sap vitality of youth. I fear for America.*

CONCLUSION

Summer camp is not supposed to be comfortable. Summer camp is supposed to be strenuous. Discomfort builds character. Scours the soul. Rasps the psyche.

Up at dawn. Cold showers. Out the doors. Reveille to Taps. Fair weather or foul. The good and vigorous life, devoid the trapping of ease.

Cal Thomas had hinted to me in our phone interview that as the decades went by, campers were beginning to balk at doing simple chores and preparing food for others. I can only imagine the issues that would be brought about with campers "needing" smart phones.

In all honesty, though, I have to tell you that I am no longer "up for" real camping trips. It wasn't ten years ago that my granddaughter Samantha received a pup tent for Christmas, and I got the bright idea to have us pitch it in my backyard and have her sleep over so we could try it out.

After we ate our raw s'mores, told stories to each other and then listened to the sounds of the night, we clicked our flashlights off and tried to sleep. That's when I realized that camping is a young person's game. Even though we both had excellent sleeping bags and foam mattresses, we both felt every root, rock and pebble for about a mile down toward the center of the earth. It was so uncomfortable that we soon abandoned the tent and camped out in the living room—me in my comfy chair and Samantha in a sleeping bag on the floor, the air-conditioner humming away all night long.

Even though I would probably need a super deluxe RV to go camping ever again, I am saddened that later generations of young people might not even want to know how much fun it can be when life is a bit of a challenge. Still, I believe there will always be children who want to swim and to sail and to ride horses and to get out into nature with their friends. Thankfully, there are still many opportunities for kids to go camping in northeast Florida. Despite the outbreak of Covid-19, some summer camps continued with shorter rosters of campers, like Immokalee, for instance, and most of the camps I visited appeared to be viable and well used, even with the difficult times that we all face.

Writing this book was a great pleasure, allowing me to explore all of the wonders of the great outdoors found in northeast Florida. My journeys had a most restorative effect on me, and I hope that traveling with me on my book's youthful romp through the northeast Florida woods provided a similar sensation to all who have ever camped and found summer camp and camping transformative.

CONCLUSION

And if, by some strange chance, you should hear the sound of "Butterfield's Lullaby" wafting in on the breeze as you turn the pages, you can be assured that it is almost time to put the lights out, go to sleep and be ready for another exciting day with the sunrise. May there be many happy camping experiences for generations to come!

BIBLIOGRAPHY

Interviews and Personal Communications

Austin, Jim. In-person interview. September 11, 2020.
Biggers, Tina Basney. Telephone interview. June 11, 2020.
Burns, Robert. Telephone interview. January 27, 2021.
Burrows, Tom. Telephone interview. July 15, 2020.
Chappell, Pamela Hutchings. Telephone interview. July 16, 2020.
Colvin, Kathy. Telephone interview. June 18, 2020.
Cressman, George. Telephone interview. October 2, 2020.
Cronin, Alex. Email message to author. November 30, 2020.
Deaver, Lesley K. Telephone interview. August 1, 2020.
Feichmeir, Margo Dovi. Email message to author. October 1, 2020.
Geer, Ranger Frank. In-person interview. October 5, 2020.
Hinely, Patrick. Email message to author. June 5, 2020.
Johnson, Mae Hotchkiss. Telephone interview. May 7, 2020.
King, Claire Fleming. Telephone interview. May 30, 2020.
Lea, Pamela. Telephone interview. May 26, 2020.
Leonard, C. Richard. Telephone interview. October 7, 2020.
Lynn, Janice. Telephone interview. May 5, 2020.
Marshall, Cal. Telephone interview. August 21, 2020.
Mathieson, Cindy. Telephone interview. May 26, 2020.
McCain, Liza. In-person interview. August 5, 2020.
Miller, David. Email message to author. May 7, 2020.

Pappas, Ted. Telephone interview. October 1, 2020.

Peacock, Rick. Telephone interview. June 1, 2020.

Redman, Jennifer. Telephone interview. May 21, 2020.

Rosenblum, Ellen Shanks. Telephone interview. May 19, 2020.

Ruland, Amanda. Telephone interview. May 20, 2020.

Rush, Brad. Telephone interview. June 17, 2020.

Sewell, Chuck E. Telephone interview. May 7, 2020.

Smith, Thomas. Telephone interview. May 7, 2020.

Watson, Judi Frazier. Telephone interview. June 10, 2020.

Articles, Books, Websites and Other Sources

AAA. "AAA School Safety Patrols Pledge." https://autoclubsouth.aaa.com/safety/aaa-school-safety-patrol.aspx.

"America the Beautiful." http://www.americathebeautiful.com/lyrics2.htm.

Anderson, R. Michael. "Summer Camp Memories: Thousands of Youngsters Have Been to Immokalee." *Florida Times-Union*, July 26, 1995.

Boy Scouts of America "Boy Scout Pledge." https://www.scouting.org/about/faq/question10.

Boy Scouts of America North Florida Council. "Camp Francis." http://www.nfcscouting.org/document/campfrancisreservation/178438.

"The Building of Camp Chowenwas [*sic*]." Jacksonville, Florida: Greater Jacksonville Council of the Girl Scouts of America, 1934.

Camp Blanding Museum. "Camp Blanding." https://campblandingmuseum.org/history.

Camp Fire. "About Camp Fire." https://campfire.org/about/.

City of Jacksonville, Florida. "Camp Tomahawk." https://www.coj.net/departments/parks-and-recreation/recreation-and-community-programming/parks/alejandro-garces-camp-tomahawk-park.aspx.

Clay County, FL. "Camp Chowenwaw Park." https://www.claycountygov.com/community/parks-and-recreation/camp-chowenwaw-park.

Delaney, Chelle. "Camp Fire Lighting Its Own Way." *Jacksonville Journal*, April 3, 1984.

Echockotee Lodge 200. "Camp Shands." https://www.echockotee.org/camp-shands-history.

Florida Times-Union. "Cub Scouts Shoot BBs." June 13, 1975.

———. List of camps in Jacksonville area. May 1, 1975.

————. "Rotary Activity Area Dedicated at Scouts' Camp Johnson." June 30, 1974.

————. "Summer Camps Periled." July 13, 1972.

Foley, Bill. "Air at Our Camp Was Conditioned, Too—By Nature!" *Florida Times-Union*, May 1, 1995.

————. "Monkey Farm's Fame Fanned Out with Hairy Arms." *Florida Times-Union*, June 5, 1988.

"Girl Scout Promise and Law." Display copy in the Camp Chowenwaw Museum.

Gould, John M. *How to Camp Out: The Original Classic Handbook on Camping, Bushcraft and Outdoors*. Eugene, OR: Doublelist Skills, 2020 (originally published in 1877).

History. "CCC (Civilian Conservation Corps)." https://www.history.com/topics/great-depression/civilian-conservation-corps.

————. "WPA (Works Progress Administration)." https://www.history.com/topics/great-depression/works-progress-administration.

Holland, Stephen W. "Boy's Special Gift Waves in Dad's Honor." *Florida Times-Union*, August 14, 1982.

Hume, Larry. "'Mr. Mont' Is Father of Camping." *Florida Times-Union*, 1981.

Hyman, Ann. "Tales of the Seaweed Witch and Popping Eyes." *Florida Times-Union*, July 7, 1994.

Jacksonville Journal. "Camp Fire Birthday." March 17, 1972.

————. "Clay Scout Camp Sold." May 1, 1979.

Kerr, Jesse-Lynn. "Echockotee Days to Remember." *Florida Times-Union*, July 14, 1974.

————. "Youth Group Sells Campsite to the Nature Conservancy." *Florida Times-Union*, July 6, 1984.

Kettles and Campfires. New York: Girl Scouts Inc., 1928.

Knight, Ray. "Days to Remember for Ex-Boy Scouts." *Jacksonville Journal*, July 6, 1973.

Let's Go Camping. Greater Jacksonville Council: Boy Scouts of America, circa 1935.

Maddox, Irene, and Rosalyn Cobb. *Campfire Songs*. Guilford, CT: FALCONGUIDES. 1983.

McMahon, Molly Brandhorst. "Amanda Petway '90 Memorial Garden." The College Today. https://today.cofc.edu/2013/06/19/amanda-petway-90-memorial-garden.

Nix, Elisabeth. "How Did 'Taps' Originate?" https://www.history.com/news/how-did-taps-originate .

"PLEASE DON'T TEAR IT DOWN!" Display copy on Big Cabin in the Camp Chowenwaw Museum.

Reed, Claire. "Summer Camp Was Just the Start." *Florida Times-Union*, July 7, 2013.

Rider, Wini. "How to Prepare for Camp." *Florida Times-Union*, May 29, 1980.

Rivoire, Alice Sanderson. *Cooking Out-of-Doors*. New York: Girl Scouts of the U.S.A., 1960.

Russell, Woody. "Camp Francis Johnson—Sale of Property Eyed." *Jacksonville Journal*, August 17, 1977.

Sing Together. New York: Girl Scout National Organization, 1936.

Sponholtz, Ann. "Y Camp '94 a Horse of a Different Color." *Florida Times-Union*, May 14, 1994.

Scouts. "St. Johns River Basin at Echockotee." https://www.scout.org/node/535154.

Tomlinson, Shellie Rushing. *Hungry Is a Mighty Fine Sauce*. Uhrichsville, OH: Shiloh Run Press, 2016.

Trammell, Nira Sue. *Front Porch Stories: Memories of Old Florida*. Privately published, 2019.

West, James E. *Scout Field Book*. New York: Boy Scouts of America, 1948.

ABOUT THE AUTHOR

*I*n 2007, Dorothy K. Fletcher retired after thirty-five years of teaching high school English in Jacksonville, Florida. At that time, she began her writing career in earnest. Along with poems, articles and novels, she wrote a monthly column for the *Florida Times-Union* called "By the Wayside," and that became the basis for the first of six histories she has written about her beloved city, Jacksonville. Presently, she and her husband, Hardy, reside in the San Jose area of Jacksonville, near their children and grandchildren, and whenever they can, they go traveling.

Left: Author as a camper at Camp Montgomery, 1964.